# Second Time Around

## Help for Grandparents
## Who Raise Their Children's Kids

Joan Callander

BookPartners
Wilsonville, Oregon

Cover design by Richard Ferguson
Text design by Sheryl Mehary

**BookPartners, Inc.**
P. O. Box 922
Wilsonville, Oregon 97071

*To my sisters Judy and Janis, who held my hand and massaged my heart back to life whenever my courage failed.*

*To Bobby, who helped Zach and me create a new life and shares our love.*

*To Mom and Dad, who love without judgment and never give up on family—and to my brother Bob for his generous gift of photography.*

*To my best friends Janet and Elvin, who are always there for me and make me laugh.*

*God gave me the special gift of family and friends and I will always be grateful.*

# Contents

# Introduction

Raising grandkids instead of retiring? Parenting when your friends are playing? You are not alone. Ten percent of American grandparents raise grandchildren for six months or longer. Increasing numbers of us are baby boomers or younger—62 percent of us are non-Latino whites; 27 percent are African-American.*

I've written this book because when I needed help, I couldn't find it. By trial and error, wasting time and money, I learned to deal with problems in a world that I didn't know existed.

I discovered juvenile hearings and criminal courts, fetal alcohol syndrome and attachment disorders. I came to terms with my daughter having four babies, each with a different father, in less than six years. I dealt with raising bail, felony convictions, custody suits, suicide and child

---

* "Money Talk," *The Oregonian,* January 16, 1997.

abuse. I got an education in AIDS testing, grandparent rights, isolation, and restructuring my life.

I wasn't young, but I was naive. Blindly, I did what authorities asked, trusting that they would do what was right. Long after I should have known better, I continued trying to help my daughter. I let logic overrule my gut feelings and didn't fight to keep my grandson from living with his natural father. My grandson will pay the price for the rest of his life.

For several years, only family, a few close friends and the women who worked for me knew what was happening in my life. Conducting business as usual was hard. One morning I had to cancel my afternoon speaking engagement in New Mexico, hours away by plane, after spending the night driving country roads and calling local hospitals without finding my daughter. She hadn't come home the night before. I was scared and embarrassed professionally and personally—I didn't know it was only a prelude to hell. Often I worked until ten at night, or came in at five in the morning to compensate for the hours I spent talking with counselors, police, attorneys and caseworkers. The seemingly endless court appearances with my daughter, and the weekly visits at Children's Services with my grandson weren't scheduled at my convenience. Sometimes, I'd shut my office door as tears rolled and mascara smeared.

Many times my staff wordlessly handed me Kleenex or listened while I talked out loud as I tried to understand, tried not to make excuses for my daughter's choices. The women I worked with were special; I could not have made it without them or my family.

I retired at the age of fifty from a large, national Yellow Pages publishing company. As directory editor, I testified in court, worked with government agencies in

Washington, D.C., and spoke with hundreds of people about birth control, adoptions, abortions and sexually transmitted diseases. My staff created the classification names for products and services and established standards for advertising content. I am now a writer and a speaker. I know where to find information and how to present it.

Slowly, I learned of others going through similar experiences. As I began to reach out and open up, I discovered only kindness and kinship. I found the more I shared, the more people sought me out. Over and over as I told my story to other grandparents, they revealed their experiences, feelings, frustrations and relief at hearing they weren't alone. There were many common experiences, including loss by theft and bad checks, having children in prison—and broken hearts. Many of our sons and daughters are drug users or alcoholics.

In chapter thirteen, I'll share other grandparents' definitions of tough love. Collectively, our rock bottom isn't the same as that of our our sons and daughters. Most grandparents feel forced into action. I vividly remember my younger sister saying, "Joan, you are going to end up raising that baby if Brandy (a fictitious name for my daughter) doesn't give it up for adoption." Adamantly I replied, "Never happen." I had talked incessantly to Brandy about the financial cost, personal sacrifices and lifelong commitment a mother must make; yet there she was—seven months pregnant, unemployed, with no baby clothes or plans for the future.

Many grandparents feel betrayed. I did. I often thought of myself and my grandchildren as innocent victims. I felt that children deserve families and I deserved freedom from responsibilities. I envied friends whose kids were married or going to college. I watched them buy trailers at the beach, vacation in Mexico, and go out to dinner. In contrast, my social highlight was a session with the counselor! Concurrently I dealt with the breakup of my seventeen-year marriage. Emotionally strung out, I lost weight, worked out at a club and tried to stay away from my house with its half-empty master closet and abandoned extra bedrooms.

Day to day you do what you have to, and when you look back as I'm doing now, six years later, you see a different person in the mirror. You are stronger. You'll probably like the person you've become. You have new roles and new rules—you are in your second parenthood.

The first chapter is based on my grandson's story. Names and minor details have been changed throughout the book to protect the privacy of all. Today, my grandson, pseudonym "Zach," is a spunky six-year-old who, a few months after being removed from his father's care, said, "Let's call my dad 'Nothing'. Then when he calls, we'll say 'How you doing, Nothing?'"

The story is an ugly story. Two men took their lives. An unborn baby died. My daughter went to prison. Zach was abused. Why am I sharing it? Because I hope it will encourage you on your journey. The letters to Zach, ending each chapter, are my heart, soul, and future legacy. As a seventy-sixth birthday present I recorded them for "Mom," my first editor, who was temporarily unable to read due to cataracts. It was a gut-wrenching experience, but strangely cathartic.

Zach's story and mine continue throughout the book, though the ensuing chapters are primarily informative. First, you are introduced to a process for making the decision about whether or not to raise your grandchild. Then come the nuts and bolts of how to get custody, keep custody, and parent effectively while maintaining adult friends and outside interests. I have tried to be conservative and consider both finances and emotions. You will find that I often make suggestions about types of experts to call and where to find them. The words "grandchild" and "grandchildren" are used interchangeably, as some raise one and some raise many.

Once you have made the decision to raise your grandson or granddaughter you must change your priorities. Your adult child no longer comes first: your grandchild is first, you are second. Last is your son or daughter. No other sequence will keep you healthy and parenting adequately. However, it is important to acknowledge that your physical and mental health are vital. Your self-care must be ongoing. If you don't care for yourself, you will be unable to care for others. You will experience irregular heartbeats this second go-round. At first there will be pain, but eventually it recedes. Then you start seeing the small blessings and you appreciate things that bring joy and happiness. You are a kinder, less judgmental person. Your life is different as a new norm emerges. Irregular is not fatal. Flexibility and creativity when faced with change, as well as a strong belief in God and a youthful attitude, are interrelated. They are all necessary if you want to be a "grand" parent.

I now have four life objectives, which you'll see reflected in my writing:

1.   *Enjoy* living, enjoy parenting and enjoy playing.

2.   *Protect* my grandson. Get him the help he needs, give him the stability and love he is entitled to, and help him become a healthy, happy adult.

3.  *Love* my daughter for who she is, not what she does. Support, do not enable. Pray for healing.

4.  *Accept* that "there's a profound difference between God allowing something to happen and God willing something to happen."*

Ordinary people doing ordinary things in a combination of usual and unorthodox ways is what this book is about. It's about attitudes, values and skills. It's a practical how-to guide designed to help you turn coping into conquering, and stress into zest.

——•——

Dear Zach,
    Life is never going to be easy for you, I know. I am sad about the pain you feel now and will throughout your life. You are special, but sometimes when we are growing up, special just feels hurtful and different. I know you will continue to be angry and sad but I hope more and more happy sneaks in and finally overshadows bad. You'll want to know why I fought for guardianship and why I seemed to let CSD place you with your dad (I didn't have a lot of control and I thought every kid deserved to feel good about their parents and live with them; I never liked your dad but I sure didn't think he would abuse you). You'll have lots of questions and will have to sift through stories from many people to arrive at the truth, because we all see it differently. I want

* 1998 Hallmark calendar quote for Tuesday, February 24.

you to know that everything I do, have done and
will do comes from loving you. From the day I
first took you home from the CSD office when
you were three years old, I was your second mom.
Only I didn't yet know it.

Grandma

# Chapter One

# Callander Story

*Courage is what it takes to stand up and speak;*
*courage is also what it takes to sit down and listen.*
— Winston Churchill

"Mom, I'm in jail," sobbed Brandy, my twenty-two-year-old daughter. Shocked, I was unaware that an avalanche of events that had started three and a half years earlier was picking up speed and would soon turn deadly.

The summer Brandy graduated from high school, she was a counselor at church camp with plans to major in law enforcement at college. One year later, she was pregnant, jobless, and living with Donald, a twenty-five-year-old construction worker she met at a party. Her savings were gone, she owed hundreds of dollars in bad checks, and my husband and I took back the car she was buying. A few months later she left Donald, saying he was mentally abusive and physically threatening. Brandy moved into a tiny camp trailer with Josh, a boy from her old high school.

It had no heat, no stove, no refrigerator and no toilet. She was pregnant with Donald's baby and sleeping with a high school senior, in a trailer with a wall-to-wall mattress.

Brandy herself is adopted, and I don't think she ever seriously considered abortion or adoption. I voiced no opinion, knowing that if I did, regardless of what decision she made, I would always be blamed if she had any regrets. I did tell her repeatedly to get a job, and a decent place to live, and start buying things for the baby or put the child up for adoption. She did nothing.

Her maternity clothes were shorts or leggings with T-shirts and grossly short sweaters. What she made, she spent. Just before her due date, Josh's mother called me complaining of marijuana use, overnight stays by other couples and unsanitary bathroom practices. Afraid my grandchild would be born with a drug addiction and no home, I called welfare and the state hospital. Brandy was furious. The state said that being poor wasn't a crime. Former friends condemned my actions and gave Brandy a baby shower. Food stamps and free medical care continued; public assistance checks started.

My husband and I had separated shortly after Brandy moved out. He had no room in his apartment and she chose not to live with me. Hurting from the pending divorce and angry with Brandy, I didn't pursue the issue. Longtime friends took Brandy into their home, for which I was grateful. Her labor lasted several days due to doctors starting and stopping medications to accommodate ebbs and flows in other deliveries. It was a nightmare. At times there were fifteen people waiting inside her hospital room or lounging outside in the stairwell. By the time my grandson Zach arrived, we were down to Brandy, her dad, Josh and me. The final birthing was exhilarating. As the baby emerged, it was fun to be the first to say "It's a boy!" I did not foresee the irony of being the one to cut the umbilical cord.

## A New Start

Brandy stayed with our friends until Zach was two months old. During that time she was clean, sober and attentive but unemployed. Determined to make it on her own, she moved into a studio apartment. Though it was in a low-income neighborhood, the rent took most of her monthly welfare check. A series of rental unit and roommate changes soon followed. Her apartments were smoke-filled and dirty, cluttered with people, pets, cigarette butts and clothes. Zach was often dressed only in diapers and a T-shirt. Nevertheless, for the most part, he appeared happy and healthy. Brandy wasn't the kind of mother I wanted her to be, but she seemed loving and adequate.

She was addicted to men and frantically looking for love. She became pregnant again—this time, the apartment manager's son was the father. Soon afterward he reconciled with his ex-wife. Brandy took Zach and moved into a house where she babysat and shared expenses with Todd, who had three children and a male lover, Dylan. Both men were HIV positive. These facts are important in understanding the tragic chain of events.

Brandy's second child was also a boy. Knowing she couldn't afford to take care of him, she helped select his adoptive parents. They met several times before the birth and waited at the hospital for his arrival. Brandy and I spent the day of her son's birth holding him and saying our lifetime hellos and goodbyes. I gave him his first bath. Later, I took him from her arms, whispering "It's time to let him go." Even now, years later, I can't see the computer screen through my tears as I relive carrying him down the hall and giving him to his new mom and dad. Periodically, Brandy showed me the photos they sent, but soon I told her it was too painful. I don't know if she is still in contact after all that has happened but I trust he is well-loved and happy.

She refused the counseling offered by the adoption agency. I asked her to stay with me for at least a few days but she went back to her place. Later, Todd claimed she told them the baby had died.

Months later, Dylan called and said Brandy was unconscious and on her way to the hospital by ambulance. I met him and Todd in the waiting room and took Zach. Brandy's dad and I alternately spent time in the emergency room with her and outside taking care of our grandson. Brandy had overdosed on phenobarbital, a prescribed medication used by Todd to control grand mal seizures. They pumped her stomach and locked her up in the mental ward. For the first but not the last time, I took Zach through secured doors to visit his mother. She told the hospital psychiatrist that she remembered having a blinding headache but not taking any pills. Shortly afterward she had her birth control implant, provided by the adoption agency, surgically removed. She did not complain of headaches after that, so maybe it was true.

Sometimes Brandy lied about the strangest things, didn't pay bills and spent diaper money on frivolous stuff. Other times she adhered to a budget and seemed to make good decisions, including enrolling in beauty school. Because she was adopted, we did not know her mental or medical heritage. I wonder if her birth mother was addicted to drugs or mentally ill.

# Physical and Tragic Endings

Todd, Dylan and Brandy were arrested in October 1994 for spanking Zach so severely on his bare buttocks and feet that he could have been seriously injured or killed.[1] The beating occurred when he refused to eat; it continued during a three- or four-hour time span. Zach was placed in the care of Children's Services (CSD). Brandy's roommates, represented by court-appointed attorneys, pled guilty to fourth-degree assault. Todd wasn't working because of his seizures and was sentenced to thirty days in jail with two years parole. His children went to live with their mother temporarily; a court custody battle had been ongoing for more than a year. Dylan had a job and was given two years probation provided he not see Todd, Todd's children, Zach or Brandy. A few days after Christmas Todd's mom called and told me Todd and Dylan had committed suicide by drinking champagne and swallowing prescription drugs. The circles of devastation were widening.

I moved Brandy in with me the night I bailed her out of jail. I insisted she start counseling immediately. Every week for an hour we played with Zach at CSD offices, in rooms with one-way mirrors and microphones. Physically, it may be a safe place for children, but it's not a safe place for hearts. I wanted to grab Zach and never let go. I wanted to tell him, "Grandma's taking you home and no one will ever hurt you again." All I could do was tell him, "I love you." I couldn't lie. Nothing was all right. Not his mom, not his being in a foster home, not my broken heart. Nothing. Visions of putting on his little coat, giving his small hand to the transportation worker and watching him walk out the door continue to haunt me. Zach was in foster care from October 1994 until March 1995 due to my ignorance.

If your grandchild is a ward of a court or if you are even thinking about involving the state, read chapter three now. Know your rights; know that the state is really many people with competing interests, and get an attorney.

Halloween, Thanksgiving, Christmas and Valentine's Day came and went. Twice we showed up for trial only to have it postponed. Brandy began staying out all night and her friends changed frequently. Attendance at beauty school was erratic even though she said she liked it. Her skin was a mass of sores; she cried easily and spent little time at the house. Finally I called my ex-husband and asked if Brandy could stay for a few weeks. I needed a break. She stayed a single night and never returned.

## Faith, Hope and Bad Tidings

My parents, seven decades wise, marched into CSD with a letter my mother had written requesting that Zach be placed with me, them, or one of my five brothers and sisters. Dad supported Mom and together they knocked down the walls that had kept Zach captive.

The little boy who came home with me was too quiet and too pale and couldn't run without falling. I held and cuddled him, started him in nursery school, and loved him with all my heart.

For months my family and my church prayed that Brandy would not be convicted of a felony or sent to jail. I was sure either would destroy any chance of employment, marriage or a future with Zach. Misdemeanors can be expunged from your record, felonies cannot. God listened and answered our prayers. Too late, I discovered it was the wrong request. Today, several years wiser, I simply pray, "God give me the strength and wisdom to know and accept your will." Had Brandy gone to jail at this point, maybe the rest of the story could have been prevented. Then again, maybe not. Destiny is not in our hands.

Brandy's attorney, also a longtime friend, not only defended her but gave her a part-time job with a promise of future job references. He succeeded in getting charges reduced to misdemeanors due in part to the fact that the two eyewitnesses were dead. No one could say which blows injured Zach. Because she was going to beauty school, working and seeing a counselor, Brandy was given probation and community service rather than jail. My daughter repaid our friend by forging his signature on a check to herself. He did not file charges; however, she was soon arrested again. This time it was for possession and distribution of a controlled substance. The police found five baggies of methamphetamines or cocaine in her jacket and a gram scale in the car she was in. I refused to post bail or attend hearings.

Pregnant for a third time, Brandy had problems. Instead of waiting in jail for her trial, she was in the state hospital because of uterine bleeding. The baby's father, the man Brandy was with when she was arrested, was sent back to prison to serve out a sentence for armed robbery. I was appalled. He had been in my home with Brandy, playing with Zach.

The infant died before birth, a common occurrence with drug mothers. It was a blessing for everyone, especially the child. Brandy was sentenced shortly afterwards but released until space opened up in prison. She worked as a waitress and lived somewhere with someone, but I've lost track of where or whom. Christmas Day 1995 was the last time I saw her for nine months. I wasn't sure if she was in jail, had left the state or was dead.

Donald, Zach's biological father, refused to take a paternity test or pay child support. It was only after the State of Alaska began garnishing his wages that he returned to Oregon, sought, and was eventually given custody of Zach. I did my best to prepare my grandson by helping him look forward to living with his father. I also told him over and over that I would always love him. The first visits were at CSD, but later Donald picked Zach up at my house. I tried to be friendly. Zach went to live with his dad in March of 1996 with the state retaining guardianship. My attorney, experienced in working with grandparents, was great. He filed for intervenor and psychological parent status and the court granted me monthly, Christmas, and summer visits. At the time I thought of it as a safety net. If things went well I wouldn't need it; however, if Donald went back to Alaska (which he talked about constantly) and abandoned Zach, or refused summer visits, I'd have legal recourse. It made Donald extremely angry, but I felt in my heart I needed to do it.

Donald seldom let Zach talk to me on the phone and every visit was a hassle. Donald had on more than one occasion been too drunk to pick up Zach after overnight visits. Zach told me his daddy "spanked" him and while doing so slapped himself on the face. I called his caseworker, who said unless there were physical marks there wasn't anything she could do. Parents can discipline their children. It was "upsetting," she volunteered, given Zach's background. She told me she knew that Donald had spanked Zach, who was barely four, for "soiling his pants." My ex-husband also called her. We were heartbroken but didn't know what to do. Zach was tense, aggressive and belligerent when he arrived on Fridays and sat crying on my lap Sundays when he had to go back. I tried teaching him my name, phone number, city and state, hoping he'd remember them if he ever needed help.

# A New Beginning

Six months after Zach was placed with his dad, Brandy phoned to say she'd been in jail. Emotionally exhausted, I agreed to meet in two weeks; however, a few days later a wedding invitation arrived in the mail. Her phone was disconnected so I dropped by the apartment listed on the return address. For the first time in years I felt optimistic. Ryan, my soon-to-be son-in-law, looked and sounded normal, and I liked him! He'd been a cook at the same restaurant for four years. They had goals and said they had known each other over a year, with Ryan standing by Brandy through her incarceration. The apartment was drab but clean. Brandy no longer had drug-induced sores all over her body. The October wedding was small, reminding me of storybook weddings in the Old West. My family, who continued to be supportive, were there, as were Ryan's. The ceremony and reception were held in a Grange hall we decorated the night before. The meal was potluck; wishes for a long and happy marriage were heartfelt.

Meanwhile, Zach's dad filed for sole custody. Brandy talked about counterfiling for joint custody. I didn't trust either of them. Donald and I had a major argument over Zach's December visit with me, which fell the weekend before Christmas. He didn't want me to see him, but I insisted. Zach and I made Christmas cookies Friday afternoon, a tradition we'd missed only the year he was in foster care. He called to me from the bathroom as I finished cleaning the kitchen. I found him standing with his hands on the floor and his bottom facing me. There were red abrasive marks on his cheeks and legs as far down as his knees. Zach said his dad hit him with a spatula after making him take down his pants and hold his ankles because "I was a bad eater." I called the abuse hotline and distracted Zach while we waited for the police. I wanted anything Zach had to say to be heard by them first.

Officer Rush arrived with toy cars and a gentle approach. He took pictures. Zach pointed to the police badge when asked the color of the spatula used by his father. Startled, I realized that it had been metal, not rubber as I imagined. Later Zach told me, "If I move he spanks me everywhere, and I moved." Zach was left in my care, pending a juvenile court hearing.

Bob (whom I'd been dating for three years), Zach, Brandy, Ryan and I drove to the mountains the next day and played in the snow. I told Brandy about the bruises and police investigation but told her to call the caseworker for details. I felt I needed to keep separate my mother and foster caretaker roles. Also, I needed to know what she would do to try to get her son back.

Sunday, Zach told Santa he wanted a train. Monday, I shopped. On Tuesday, Christmas Eve, Zach was examined by doctors at Emanuel Hospital, where he repeated his story and his fears. I spent several hours in a deserted waiting room and didn't keep the Christmas stocking they gave him after it was emptied of candy, small toys and books. Some memories you don't want to memorialize.

Zach still doesn't want to see Donald, calling him a "bad dad." He often says things like "Remember when I was good enough that you came and got me." Donald refused to cooperate with CSD. He missed the juvenile hearing, claiming when the judge called him that he had car trouble. There had already been two postponements in order that he might retain a lawyer.

# Family and Future

Years ago, Brandy was my first priority. The day Zach moved in with me, he became Number One. I wanted Zach and Brandy back together as mother and son; however, I eventually sued for custody after finding out she was pregnant again. On Zach's fifth birthday, while he romped through SuperPlay's plastic tunnels, Brandy and I talked. We agreed that it was critical to his recovery for him not to have to compete for attention with a baby until he was feeling loved and secure. After becoming pregnant, she insisted that she and her husband's sex life was their business. I couldn't have agreed more. However, sex wasn't the issue—but Brandy didn't get it.

Zach was an angry, scared little boy. His counselor identified him as emotionally a two-and-a-half-year-old child, although chronologically he was five. He kicked, screamed, ran from the house, broke furniture and hit. He kept me in his sight, needing constant hugs, kisses and reassurance. Getting him to sleep often took hours. Zach required one-on-one parenting. Anything less would put Brandy's new baby and Zach at risk physically.

I was given permanent custody and guardianship, but I wasn't the answer to Zach's prayers. Zach is God's gift to me. Brandy and I are still trying to making things work. She too was a special gift. I fell in love with her many years ago in a small-town hospital.

Writing this chapter has been painful. I did it with the hope of helping others overcome feelings of isolation, guilt and embarrassment for things their children have done.

Remember—"A person without dreams can never be motivated."[2] Your grandchildren are young enough to dream. You are just the right age to motivate. That's why this book is about deciding to be better, not bitter.

— • —

Dear Zach,

I cried so hard that I sank to the floor where I'm writing this, too heartsick to get up and too scared of what's going to happen, to sleep. I can't stop seeing you with your blond curls, dressed in your little Levi's and the red plaid flannel shirt I bought you. Bob says I kept saying over and over "He's just a baby, he's just a baby," but I don't even remember. The biggest horror to me is that your mom doesn't seem sorry or appalled by what she did. She's angry because the CSD worker represented himself (she felt) as a sheriff and she wants to talk to Todd. Who cares! They spanked you for several hours—for God's sake—on your bottom and tops of your feet. I'll call Jake tomorrow (he's an attorney and our friend) and CSD. I pray to God you are safe tonight wherever you are and aren't afraid.

Love,
Grandma

# Chapter Two

# To Parent or Not to Parent?
# That Is the Question

*"And what is as important as knowledge?"*
*asked the mind.*
*"Caring," answered the heart.*

—Flavia Weede

"Are you in or are you out?"

In poker, every time the ante raises, all players must decide if they are willing and able to continue. Willingness is commitment. Ability is resources. Making the decision to raise grandchildren or to step aside requires a *willingness* to live with the consequences of your choice regardless of how the cards may fall in the future. It also requires the *ability* to follow through with your choice.

*Not making a decision is making a decision, without allowing yourself the opportunity to influence the outcome.*

Children need parenting. They need it every day of their lives, not just when their parents are ready. Raising grandchildren is demanding. The parent-child-grandchild triangle is stressful at best, and ugly at its worst. Raising children is costly and physically demanding. "Hardside love is doing what's best for another person regardless of the cost. Held in balance, it's the ability to be consistent, to discipline, to protect, to challenge and to correct."[1]

If you can't provide the home, discipline and love your grandchildren need, you must accept their living with natural, foster or adoptive parents. Having adopted my daughter, who gave up a son for adoption, I am convinced that stepping out of someone's life may be the most selfless act of love we can offer. Raising grandchildren, or supporting removal from their parents, doesn't mean you don't want their mom or dad to accept the responsibility. We all want our children to be reliable, caring and successful adults. Your decision acknowledges that it isn't going to happen, or at least not for many months or years. Some grandparents assume legal, as well as physical custody, others co-parent with sons or daughters, and others offer interim homes, intervene sporadically or support foster placement or adoption. There is a lot to consider before reaching a decision.

Many of us thought this would be our Miller time. We envisioned few family or financial responsibilities. We wanted to work out, eat out and live out our dreams. Dreams included babysitting our grandchildren when we wanted, buying I Love Grandma T-shirts when vacationing and getting on with growing old. Changing diapers, buying braces, carpooling and counseling weren't in the dream. So, as the Oregon State Lottery advertises, "Adjust your dreams accordingly." Can you picture yourself happily enjoying pizza and high school football, jogging while pushing a stroller or sending care packages to college? Trying to decide what's best for you and your grandchildren requires thought, planning and prayer (good friends who are willing to listen and share a glass of wine don't hurt). "Just Do It" doesn't work.

### Feelings are facts—do not minimize yours

"Willing" is a decision of the heart, "able" is a decision of the mind. For many grandparents there is no meeting of their minds and hearts. "There's someone at the door, you'll have to call back," said Ruby, an elderly African-American grandma raising her daughter's five children. When my questions got too painful, she'd hang up the phone. "For her, it's an effort just to keep a roof over their heads and see that they make it to school," confided a mutual acquaintance.

Nine years ago Ruby spent twenty-four months rounding up grandchildren from various foster homes in California. The youngest one, Johnny, has been with her since he was two days old. His mother is in and out of their lives. He saw his father, who overdosed on drugs, just once. It was the same day he met his paternal grandparents—they had taken him to his father's funeral. He doesn't know his maternal grandfather either. "Them or me," his grandfather had said to his grandmother. Her actions shouted back, "Them!" but you can still feel her heart crying, "All of you."

The process of writing down information gathered by using your head and listening to your heart is important. It clarifies feelings and increases awareness. Later, it will help in setting boundaries, establishing goals, and maintaining control of your life. If you are married or if you have a significant other, the following exercise should be shared. Depending on personalities and decision-making styles, you may prefer testing it individually and then discussing the results. It is usually easier to be objective about information gathered through your five senses than through your heart.

Admitting feelings is tough. Acting on feelings is even tougher. Answering the following questions will help you sort things out. Then it will be easier to make your decision and live with it.

### 1.  Myself

*Health*

    Do I have a terminal or degenerative illness?    Yes   No

    Do I have physical limitations?    Yes   No

    Am I able to hear and pick up a crying baby or toddler?    Yes   No

    Can I protect myself and/or restrain my grandchild?    Yes   No

*Religion*

    Church is important to me.    Yes   No

    My grandchild shares my faith.    Yes   No

*Finances*

    My income will cover increased expenses.    Yes   No

    I will get adequate supplemental income from parents/government.    Yes   No

| | | |
|---|---|---|
| My insurance covers the child. | Yes | No |
| There is space in my home. | Yes | No |
| I can afford preschool or after school care. | Yes | No |
| I can help with college. | Yes | No |
| My existing car is adequate or I live near a bus/transit line. | Yes | No |
| I can afford legal fees. | Yes | No |

*Custody*

| | | |
|---|---|---|
| I will have legal custody. | Yes | No |
| I will have court-appointed physical custody. | Yes | No |
| If there are no legal safeguards, can I live with the fact that my son or daughter has the right to reclaim my grandchild at some future date? | Yes | No |

## 2.   Grandchildren

*Health*

| | | |
|---|---|---|
| Are they physically healthy? | Yes | No |

*Education*

| | | |
|---|---|---|
| Is their grade level age-appropriate? | Yes | No |

| | | |
|---|---|---|
| Is tutoring or special help needed? | Yes | No |

*Attitudes*

| | | |
|---|---|---|
| Do they want to live with me? | Yes | No |
| Do they want to see their parent(s)? | Yes | No |
| Are there gang or drug problems? | Yes | No |

## 3. Parents

| | | |
|---|---|---|
| Do they abuse drugs or alcohol? | Yes | No |
| Is a recovery probable? | Yes | No |
| Is either in jail? | Yes | No |
| Is either deceased? | Yes | No |
| Do they have mental or physical problems? | Yes | No |
| Do they have financial or marital problems? | Yes | No |
| Do mother and father live together? | Yes | No |
| If not, is there contact by both? | Yes | No |
| Do the parent(s) call or visit regularly? | Yes | No |
| Do the parent(s) live with me? | Yes | No |

| | | |
|---|---|---|
| If yes, will they continue to? | Yes | No |

*Attitudes*

| | | |
|---|---|---|
| Will they fight for custody? | Yes | No |
| Do they sabotage my efforts with the child? | Yes | No |

**4.   Other players**

| | | |
|---|---|---|
| Do state caseworkers, counselors, attorneys and judges support me? | Yes | No |
| Does my spouse or partner support me? | Yes | No |
| Do extended family and friends support me? | Yes | No |

Still with me? Good. You probably noticed that all sections had attitude or feeling questions except the first. Now that you've practiced identifying feelings that you've observed in others, it will be easier to do it for yourself.

**5.   My feelings**

| | | |
|---|---|---|
| I can separate my anger at my son or daughter from my feelings for my grandchildren. | Yes | No |
| I have the patience to handle their special needs. | Yes | No |

| | | |
|---|---|---|
| I am willing to maintain contact with my son or daughter. | Yes | No |
| I am willing to stop all contact with my son or daughter. | Yes | No |
| I am willing to make new friends that we both will enjoy. | Yes | No |
| I want to raise my grandchild. | Yes | No |
| I am willing to make a lifetime commitment. (If not, for how long?)_____ | Yes | No |
| I am the best person to raise my grandchild (love is not the issue). | Yes | No |

If you still can't make a decision, the timing simply isn't right. In the meantime, keep reading, keep praying and give your troubles to God. He'll be up all night anyway.

—●—

Dear Zach,

We're blessed with family! I couldn't make it without them. They sit in court and listen for hours while I vent and you sleep. They drop off little surprises like glow stars for your ceiling so you won't be afraid of the dark. Never do they judge or condemn. They also don't let me wallow in the "pity pools" of life, nor do they just throw out life preservers. Nope, they jump right in and hold me up.

Aunt Judy has been my unpaid counselor for years and is my best friend in the whole world. Aunt Janis is always, always, always there for us. Remember all the cookies we've baked together as I took those frustratingly stupid foster parenting classes (or a weekend break here and there)? Great Grandma Betty wrote a letter and with Great Grandpa Johnny (not many people want to cross him!) marched right into the CSD office and demanded that they let you live with me or one of the family. Your uncles keep us in their prayers and help in their own special ways. I wish with all my heart that someday you and your sister Cher will track down your adopted half brother and all become friends—because that's what a family is—forever friends.

Hugs,
Grandma

# Chapter Three

# Working Through the System

*We cannot expect people to do what we would do, unless they know what we know.*
—Charles Coonradt and Jack Lyon, and Richard Williams, *Managing the Obvious*

## Quick Tips

- If the state has legal or physical custody, get an attorney.

- The state considers you a poor risk because you raised your children, and look how they turned out. Every statement you make, backed by every action, must put the needs of your grandchild first. Then you will be considered a resource.

- Learn the right people to call and the right questions to ask.

- Call your senators and representatives, and TV, radio and newspaper reporters with your story, if state agencies are unresponsive or out of line.

# Attorneys

Attorneys know the key players in state agencies and the judicial system. They know the law and your options, including your rights as psychological parent, intervenor or grandparent.

They know the courtroom presentation style most effective for each judge. My friend who represented my daughter told me he has spent days sitting in courtrooms observing judges before critical trials. What works with one judge could blow you out of the water with another.

Never hire an abrasive attorney. They hurt your case, especially in juvenile court where many decisions are highly subjective. Recommendations of caseworkers, counselors, child advocates and district attorneys are highly valued by the judge who decides your grandchild's fate. Negotiations out of court save both time and money.

Lawyers can objectively evaluate the facts as they relate to the law because they are not emotionally involved. If they say your odds are not good and you decide to quit, don't feel guilty. If they say your odds are excellent and you decide to quit, don't feel guilty either. Legal fees can quickly wipe out life savings, but stress can destroy your health. If God wants you to continue, He'll keep things stirred up.

For more than two and a half years I vacillated between wanting to parent Zach and wanting to be "free." Every time I thought I knew what God wanted me to do, another curve ball was thrown. The day of the final custody hearing, I arrived at the courthouse so early that the hallways were empty. My steps echoed on the old worn marble tile as I walked and prayed, hoping I wasn't making a horrible mistake.

It wasn't until the guardianship papers were signed that peace finally came into my life and I felt all right as a mother. I became ten years younger. Suddenly, it was okay not to dress in suits and go to an office; it was okay to have sticky kitchen floors; okay to be working on my book at midnight.

Legally and emotionally, you will have an uphill battle. Parental rights supersede child's best interest in most states. Parents often have court-appointed attorneys who, even if overworked and inexperienced, are far more effective than no attorney. You need to legally ensure the physical safety and future custody of your grandchildren. Otherwise, you'll be in court or your grandchildren will be back with their parents every time your son or daughter cycles through clean and sober phases.

"Learn how to detach so you aren't in pain all of the time" is one grandparent's suggestion. Others simply refuse to get involved a second or third time.

# Government

Government takes hard-working, caring, dedicated people and makes them crazy. The structure and size of the system, not lack of caring, cause ineptness and heartache. Every agency or department has different and often conflicting interests. Caseworkers and court-appointed attorneys have budget problems and need to reduce caseloads. District attorneys want criminal convictions. Foster parents and mental health providers get paid per child.

It's a dysfunctional conglomerate. Never assume information is shared. Repeat critical facts, emotions, and concerns to everyone.

"If it takes a beating with a two-by-four to get the child's attention that's what you use," stated Janee's son-in-law in a pretrial conference. The district attorney and the caseworker were late due to traffic, but Janee made sure they heard and understood the importance of the statement. A pretrial conference is where attorneys and clients try to iron out differences without judge or jury present. The hearing that day was postponed, because the son-in-law claimed his attorney was unavailable.

Two months later she repeated that statement to the new caseworker, before the rescheduled hearing date. She told the district attorney as they were gathering outside the courtroom. That hearing was also postponed. The father said he had to find a lawyer. She reminded the caseworker and her granddaughter's attorney three months later. She told her attorney, and she told the district attorney who was filling in for the original district attorney. All of them had forgotten, or weren't involved when the remark was made. It had no bearing on the guilt or innocence of the father in the physical abuse hearing, but it may have moved the players to fight harder to keep her grandchild safe with her.

Repeat important details just before court hearings. Be prepared to bring them out yourself in testimony. Write down everything. You will forget dates and details unless you do.

## Adult and Family Agencies

Family and child welfare agencies are large bureaucracies, managed by political appointees, that long ago lost the ability to do the logical, the expedient, the practical or the humane. Most of these agencies are charged with reuniting families. This makes them parent advocates. Your grandchild's parents need be only minimally functional to keep or regain custody.

Caseworkers are tremendously overworked and burned out. Social services are known for rapid turnover. Therefore, they may never know your child's history from start to finish. There isn't time for the original caseworker to document events adequately or for new ones to read everything.

Inexperienced caseworkers give bad advice with good intentions. They believe in the system, parent recovery, and maybe even Santa Claus. They have limited authority and stick to the rule book. Question everything and press for answers! Immediately appeal adverse decisions, or lack of progress, to office or district managers. The higher the management, the more responsive they are to media, legal, or political intervention.

"Call, write, or visit everyone you think might help," one grandmother told me as she wiped her hands on her paint-smeared jeans and moved aside a pile of cedar shakes for the Victorian home she'd been building herself for eight years. The house overlooked the Willamette River a half-mile below. She focused on the river as she paced back and forth across the unfinished flooring. Struggling to keep her frustration in check, she told me about the most recent conversation. "For fourteen months I've done all the calling. They don't even ask to talk with Macy to make sure she is all right. They certainly don't care about me." More than a year earlier, Idaho CSD had begun cashing and with-holding the money from Macy's Social Security checks, the only benefit bequeathed by a dad who died by drug overdose. Margaret told the supervisor that she would write to legislators in both states to make that stop. Because Idaho had legal guardianship, the supervisor felt it was irrelevant that the agency spent none of Macy's money for her upkeep. He, like the caseworker, suggested that Margaret hire an attorney and adopt her granddaughter.

Margaret doesn't want an attorney or adoption. She wants her daughter to get off drugs and take care of her grandchild. Her mood changes from frustration to anger. Margaret, who carried the Olympic torch over the Oregon-Washington interstate bridge when she was a forty-one-year-old grandma back in 1984, seldom gets angry. She showed me copies of the letters she'd written asking, "Why is a state agency receiving benefits for a child they do not have? Sometimes going to the newspaper and/or media helps these situations, is that what I should be doing?" Two weeks later a jubilant Margaret called to tell me, "They are mailing all of Macy's back money and we've got a new caseworker."

Experienced caseworkers are jewels. They don't break rules, but they will look for alternatives when routine answers don't make sense. Caseworkers visit the week after placement and the week before hearings. Children will be atypically good or bad, so be prepared. Tell caseworkers the behavior the child normally exhibits. A brief log with dates, quotes, and incidents really helps.

Parent-child reunification may be authorized if parents "pass" psychological evaluation, test negative for alcohol or drug use, attend parenting classes and demonstrate means of support (including welfare). If parent-child reunification occurs, there is little follow-up. The state tolerates physical discipline by mothers and fathers, even when the children have been abused, unless there are visible bruises, scars or other signs of injury. Children are interviewed at home, if at all, so they seldom complain—because they are afraid or act out of misguided loyalty.

On the other hand, you will be thoroughly investigated before you are given temporary physical custody if the state has intervened. If you are accepted as a foster care provider, even if the foster child is your grandchild, the child qualifies for mental and dental insurance, and health care. In addition, you will receive a set monthly expense check in an amount determined by the age of the child—not by your expenses.

With foster care come mandatory orientation and parenting classes, extensive paperwork, home visits, and requirements such as fire extinguishers and a lock on your medicine cabinet. Background and reference checks will be done on all adults in your home. The parent from whom your grandchild was removed must have a low income. Your financial situation is not an issue unless the foster payment is your primary or only income—which could disqualify you.

In most instances, it is easiest to ask for "relative placement" and then apply through Adult Family Services (AFS), a state agency, for "non-needy relative assistance." Then neither your income nor the parents' is a consideration.

Mental health counseling services under most private plans have limited lifetime caps as well as hefty copayments. AFS insurance does not. Most grandchildren need, or will need, counseling for parental abuse, grief, drugs, abandonment, adjustment to co-parenting or other issues. Check your insurance benefits. You also receive a small monthly check that you can use for daily expenses or save for college or emergencies. The downside is completing ongoing government paperwork, as you must reapply frequently.

# Court-Appointed Attorney
# Special Advocate (CASA)

The court-appointed attorney or special advocate for your grandchild has the responsibility for looking out for the child's best interest. Most work hard as your grandchild's protector and ally. Their job is to ensure that your grandchild gets counseling, medical services, educational benefits and the best possible temporary and permanent placement. Attorneys often work for nonprofit, public-interest law firms that contract with states or counties for their services. The CASA is a specially trained volunteer who works with one or two children. Be open and honest in sharing information. Demonstrate that you place your grandchild's best interest above your own or that of their parents.

If your attorney or CASA is not active or effective, ask the court to appoint another one. CASA and the court are resources for selecting your own attorney. Ask them to recommend attorneys who are experienced in grandparents' rights. Yellow Pages, bar associations and referral agencies are also resources.

Always interview prospective attorneys and talk to prior clients if you or your friends know them. Personally, I want an ethical attorney with a history of winning cases— one who is recommended by clients and peers and who charges reasonable fees.

# Mental Health Counselors

Counselors are empathetic, caring individuals; but they are often overworked, sometimes burned out, with a professional obligation to protect the privacy of their clients. This means that unless your grandchild gives permission, anything said to them will not be repeated to you. They can give you suggestions and apprise you of overall progress. If your counselor is also a parent or has intensive experience with children, he or she can help save your sanity. If your grandchild or you do not relate well, ask to be reassigned. Not every relationship works.

Counselors talk in English but testify in Academic, which does not paint strong, emotional pictures for judges or juries. Always, always, always have your attorney question counselors in advance about exactly what they will say to tough questions under oath. Ask each question many times with slight variations to make sure they will be consistent, convincing and supportive. Your attorney may want to substitute psychological evaluations and testimony from forensic experts, who routinely appear in court and present themselves and information effectively.

I was fortunate that Zach had a counselor who spoke passionately, from her heart. She described his needs vividly once my attorney explained the need for clarity and conviction—not clinical nomenclature. I don't remember her testimony exactly, but I heard her whisper to herself as she left the courtroom, "I did my best for you, Zach."

Over and over she had told me, "Zach needs peace and quiet twenty-four hours a day. Zach has to have calm, stable parenting." Children like Zach, if they can't attach to someone, may become the violent criminals we see so often today. I remember the day I finally understood what I heard. That was the day I went ballistic as I understood the enormous responsibility and commitment necessary to parent Zach.

I broke up with my boyfriend that night without telling him why. Luckily, a little sanity returned the next day, and when I explained that I needed to be a twenty-four-hour-a-day full-time mom for the next thirteen to sixteen years, he simply said, "I'll be there. I love him too; even if we had broken up, I was going to ask you if I could still see him. He's in my heart." Doesn't God give us miracles just when we need them?

This all happened two days before I left for a vacation in Maui with my zany friend Janet. It would be the last I could afford for a long time, but it gave me the time to quietly gather strength as Janet forced me to laugh. That vacation was the first time either of us had flown in a heli-copter—a real test of courage for Janet, who is afraid of heights, and for me (I am afraid of nearly everything). It was sort of a test run.

When we got back Janet found out she had cancer. And I had to battle my daughter. We were both fighting for life.

# District Attorneys

Most district attorneys are overworked or starting careers with plans to go into private practice or politics, so there is constant turnover. As they juggle court appearances, colleagues may fill in for them, so valuable information is lost. Make sure your attorney or caseworker or your grand-child's attorney helps bring new players up to speed. Court postponements are the norm, so expect many.

# Courts and Related Information

*Domestic and criminal court*

Criminal charges against parents are heard in criminal court. Juvenile hearings don't result in criminal convictions or sentences for abuse, drug charges or criminal neglect, for adults. Domestic issues, such as guardianship, custody and visitations, are heard in a domestic court of law. Juvenile and civil hearings may be consolidated, but not criminal hearings.

### *Juvenile court*
A judge or a referee presides, determining if the state can obtain and/or continue legal custody and if the physical placement of the child in the state's custody is appropriate.

## Dressing for and Testifying in Court

First impressions are lasting. They are strongly based on your appearance. Communication experts estimate that the first seven to fifteen seconds of what you say is not heard.

* Dress conservatively in classic color combinations such as navy, black, tan, wine, camel, forest green or gray. These suggest stability, loyalty, and respectability. However, whether you are a man or woman, add at least one softening touch, such as a pastel or colorful scarf, loafers, or a sweater rather than a jacket.

* Don't wear flashy jewelry, high-heeled shoes, plunging necklines, black leather or anything that does not look like a grandparent leaving for church.
* Chewing gum in the courtroom or smoking where you can be seen creates a negative image.

* Avoid strong fragrances in aftershave or perfume.

- Never be abrasive, condescending, or flippant.

- Body language is as important as what you say in words. Make eye contact with the judge, jury, district attorney and other key players—especially when you are speaking. Don't wring your hands, play with your hair or cross your arms in front of your body.

- Emotion will not be harmful to your case as long as it is honest and held in check. If you start to cry, ask for a minute to regain your composure. If you are angry, say so, but explain why in rational, nonthreatening words and calm tones. A grandparent who conveys love, caring and concern through emotion as well as words is more believable.

- Family members or friends are an extension of you. If their dress, speech, attitude or personality negates, or sends mixed messages, leave them home.

- When testifying, answer one question at a time. Ask attorneys or judges to rephrase, or say something like "The answer to your first question is…". Some attorneys combine questions, hoping that you will become confused or rattled. If you don't understand a question, say so.

- If someone inaccurately quotes or paraphrases you correct them. "I didn't say," "You misunderstood," or "Let me restate what I said" are all effective ways to call attention to the mistake and correct the court records. Letting something slide may harm you later in this or another hearing.

- If asked the same question in slightly different ways, repeat the same answer. Calm and consistent responses are important. The opposing attorney is trying to get you to contradict yourself or react emotionally.

- Be yourself, and speak to the person asking the question rather than give a rehearsed speech. In juvenile court it is permissible to ask the judge if you may make additional comments.

- The system is a costly, time-consuming place to be in; however, try to work with the people and they will, in turn, be as honest and helpful as they can. Most would not be doing what they are today if they didn't love and want to help children.

—•—

Dear Zach,

This is tough. I got you ready and took you to great grandma and grandpa's in between running to the bathroom. When I get scared or nervous I have to go to the bathroom. I went to court and told the judge why I didn't think your mommy can keep you safe. I didn't want to tell him. I didn't want to hurt your mommy. You see, in my heart she's still my little girl. But I had to. I had to keep you safe and your unborn sister safe. When you are angry you are violent. Remember when Bobby was lying on his side on the floor and you kicked him so hard he collapsed or when you shook your rocking chair until the arm broke? Well, what if that was your baby sister? I don't want her

dead or a vegetable with brain damage and I
would die if they took you away and locked you up
in an institution or juvenile jail. With time and
counseling and one-on-one attention, I know
someday you'll be the happy, smiley Zach that you
were before all this awful stuff started.

You are my "freetie" (those "esses" were so
hard for you to say),

Grandma

# Chapter Four

# My God Is an Awesome God

*God, grant me the serenity to accept*
*the things I cannot change,*
*courage to change the things I can,*
*and the wisdom to know the difference.*
—Serenity Prayer

We all need a Higher Authority to believe in as much
as we need air to breathe. What we call our Maker doesn't
matter—God, Jehovah, Buddha, Mother Earth. It matters
that we believe, that we pray and that we lead an ethical life.
It matters to our earthly sanity, our happiness and health. It
matters to our eternal soul. It's the gift of life for our grandchildren.

For centuries people lived together in castles, tribes
and small villages sharing housing, work, religious beliefs
and rituals. Personal boundaries were honored and commu-
nities took care of their own. Today's families live in a
sprawling "urbania" with drive-by and freeway shootings

invading our personal space. Employers and employees no longer have lifetime commitments or mutual respect. Divorce is rampant. There is no day of worship set aside for honoring God. Physically and spiritually, we live in isolation created by television, videos, telecommuting, Internet shopping and bars on the windows of houses, apartments and hearts.

I've come to understand the importance of ritual to spirituality and the joy found in religion. If going to church is a duty that drains your energy rather than feeding it, find another church. Help, peace and hope for the future are God's promises to us if we are willing to search.

Seven years ago, newly divorced and with a daughter on drugs, I needed more than the down-and-dirty 7:30 A.M. mass that I had grown up attending. For me it had become a "fast food" religious experience. Cheap, fast and easy, it cost me little and nourished me not at all. I found my answer at Rolling Hills, an evangelical church where music is intricately interwoven with Bible study and family counseling. For a year I cried my way through most services, but as the pain oozed out, God crept in. Religion is personal and I'm not selling mine; I just want to share the comfort of belief.

Miami Dolphins coach Don Shula attends mass daily. He explains in his book *Everyone's a Coach* that it's his time to thank God, ask for help and listen for answers. He draws strength from the same services that put me on automatic pilot. His football successes flash across the nation's television screens most Monday nights in the fall. In my opinion, they are not half as impressive as his inclusion in a book by Peggy Stanton, *The Daniel Dilemma: The Moral Man in the Public Arena,* which features nine men who live their faith even at personal cost. Spirituality is belief in a supreme being. Religion is our approach to that supreme being. God hears us all.

God doesn't make mistakes: there is a divine reason for everything. No prayer goes unanswered. But heavenly justice is not human justice nor is His timing our timing. When you accept these truths, you stop worrying. You can hand over problems to God and walk away trusting that He will solve them. In her tape series, "Energy Anatomy: The Science of Personal Power, Spirituality and Health," Dr. Caroline Myss, medical intuitive, tells listeners that the best way to make God laugh is to tell Him our plans. I'm sure He's gotten some real guffaws over mine.

The rest of this chapter is my personal collection of "aha-ha's." In it, you may find something that makes you laugh, brings you peace or helps you to help a child.

- I need a "Just-Do-It" God.

- God's plan may be to destroy your plans until you fall in line with His plans.

- Emergencies in our life are not emergencies in God's life.

- "What is your life? You are a mist that appears for a little while and then vanishes."
  —James 3:15

- Sometimes you have to help a friend cry.

- Your life will be guided by either fear or faith.

- "Religion is a candle inside a multicolored lantern. Everyone looks through a particular color, but the candle is always there."
  —Mohammed Negulb

- Life isn't fair. Get over it!!

- You'll be a happier person if you quit trying to judge everything as good or bad. Make room for future changes.

- Being the best you can be honors God and inspires others.

- As long as the moon shall rise,
  As long as the rivers shall flow,
  As long as the sun shall shine,
  As long as the grass shall grow.
  —Expression found in Native American treaties

- "Don't compromise yourself. You are all you've got."
  —Janis Joplin

- "Everything is permissible for me—but not everything is beneficial."
  —I Corinthians 7:31

- Have you ever noticed that, broken apart, the word "message" is really an abbreviated way of saying life can be a mess at any age?

- Not everything is solved in this life.

- "A force has always led me back home, and straightened out my course in life."
  —Wolfman Jack

- "How can we trust you? When Jesus Christ came on earth, you killed him and nailed him to a cross."
  —Chief Tecumseh, 1810

- Prayer doesn't stop the consequences of doing wrong.

- When all else fails, share a margarita with a friend.

- "It is no use walking anywhere to preach unless our walking is our preaching."
  —St. Francis of Assisi

- Don't you just hate it when you get a second chance to do the wrong thing?

- It's our job to do the right thing and God's job to take care of the consequences.

- "I am awake."
  —Buddha

- You don't have to be afraid of tomorrow because God is already there.

If you don't go to church for yourself, do it for your grandchildren. All is not right with their world. Their family is different and that is a truth that we are powerless to change. If their need for validation, ritual and community is not met by religion, it will be filled by joining gangs, using drugs, or other self-destructive behaviors. Thought by thought, deed by deed, and prayer by prayer we can give our kids not only a heritage but a future built on values, not violence.

—•—

Dear Zach,

I learn so much from you. You are my little miracle. I agree, "Hugs and Kisses" is a much better way to end a prayer than "Amen," and I'm sure God is smiling. I'm sorry that I yelled at you today. I know that it scares you. I'd know even if you didn't cover your ears. Tomorrow we'll go shopping for a dreamcatcher.

Hugs and sweet dreams,
Grandma

# Chapter Five

# Been There. Done That. Doing It Differently.

*How we change as we grow—rearrange what we know.*

—LaVyrle Spenser
*Small Town Girl*

Raising grandkids is not Life 101. It's at least master's level and probably doctoral work. It's tough. Infants, toddlers, juveniles and teens all have problems. We are older, and technology and drugs have altered the world. "Global village" is an oxymoron. There are no shared goals or values. What you teach at home is under continual siege by today's music, movies, news, gangs and drug dealers. Teachers, coaches, and other parents, as well as kids' peers, often unknowingly add to the assault. Everyone is willing to tell you what you are doing wrong, or how to do it better, but they aren't there when the kids take the car without permission, throw things because they are angry or spend the day waiting for a mom or dad who never come.

What skills and approaches to parenting do you need to help you and your grandchild survive and thrive? According to teachers, counselors and caseworkers, second-time-around parents' greatest strengths include flexibility, calmness in crisis, willingness to solve problems without placing blame, a realistic outlook on life, and inner strength.

"I could just kick his butt," said Lydia, waving a spatula over the large outdoor grill where she fries eggs for fourteen adults. Our daughters had played high school soccer together and she and her husband Jack were the youth leaders at St. Anne's. Anyone who didn't know her wouldn't see how worried she is, but they've gotten a call from Sam, their seventeen-year-old nephew, and she has quietly begun closing up their cabin on the mist-covered canal.

I'd watched for years as they reorganized their life. They raised two daughters while trying to help Lydia's alcohol-addicted sister, Karen, and parent her two children. They had driven miles through heavy traffic every Monday morning to pick up Karen at her apartment and bring her back to work in the machine shop they operated in their garage. Often they came back alone. They paid to have her rotting teeth fixed and they paid for family interventions. Finally, ten years ago they went to court and took in Sam and his sister Stormy, and they stopped being caregivers for Karen. The children followed them around like puppies. Jack spent his days at work and his nights at soccer games or under the hoods of racing cars with Sam.

Last night, Sam drove his older cousin home and was pulled over by the police. There was alcohol in the truck. Sam hadn't been drinking, but the police impounded the pickup. "He has a smart mouth," said Jack. "Sometimes police can be hard on kids We need to go hear his story."

The sun was barely up, but the weekend was over and the weariness was back. Grandparents and other relatives who parent for a second time know most things are not black or white. There are many versions of the truth. There are many paths to the same destination.

### Focus on strengths

Everyone has natural aptitudes as well as likes and dislikes. Don't waste time strengthening weaknesses or beating yourself up over things you hate. Self-discipline is not a solution. I'm not even sure it's a virtue. Delegate tasks. Say no. Change priorities. Lower standards—perfectionism can be a form of procrastination. Get on with the things you do well. As Mother Teresa noted, "The greatest disease today is not leprosy or tuberculosis, but rather the feeling of being unwanted, uncared for and deserted." Being Mom or Dad is the most underrated and important job in the universe. Being a stand-in mom or dad is even more critical. There is no such thing as being "just a homemaker." You are preparing human beings to take their places in society. What you teach will be passed on to their children and live for generations to come. You are ensuring the continuity of the universe and God's plans.

### Ask for help

Call a neighbor, ask a schoolmate's parents, contact your local retired executives' association, inquire at church, plead with family or solicit help from local businesses. Ask people to mentor, tutor, coach, babysit, entertain or work with your grandchild. "It would mean a lot to me" is hard to ignore. You'll find that if you ask for a little, people give a lot.

*Barter*

Offer to trade time. Run errands, bake bread, build decks, design brochures, become the carpool king or queen. Do whatever is necessary to expose your grandchildren to new experiences or help them develop skills. Sometimes, your only objective may be free time for yourself.

*Pay for services*

Don't want to run alongside a bike, kick a soccer ball, or help with the science project? Pay a junior or senior high school student to do it for you. Ask a niece, nephew or family friend to supervise (for a fee) shopping for youngsters or teens. Discuss limits and expectations in advance so they don't overspend or shock you with their choices. They'll avoid gang colors, stoner's attire and nerd wear while shopping for what's "in" at the lowest price. Clothes, makeup and hair are among the first areas in which kids start exerting independence. Give high school students a budget, drop them off at the mall, and let them make their own choices. Don't supplement if the money runs out— handling money is half the lesson. There is a double generation gap between your ideas and your grandchild's. Prepare yourself and try to be supportive. Better to look foolish at thirteen than at thirty.

*Take in foreign exchange students*

Not my idea but I love it—handpicked surrogate brothers or sisters! Carolmae and her husband always request someone with younger siblings at home, who has the sports skills and family values they want modeled. Good grades are mandatory. They help the exchange student get an American driver's license, and the student in turn takes their grandson Marty to school and social events. In the past three years he has learned to snowboard, skateboard and play soccer.

His grandparents like having young people in the house. Carolmae, alias "Mom," laughs as her husband, who has been retired for two years, emerges from the bedroom still buttoning his pants. "Not walking through the house naked or in my briefs was the hardest adjustment when Marty moved in," he grins. Carolmae continues, "We'd been without kids for over twelve years. You have to rethink vacations, and eating out—you know, the obvious things. I love being home. Having young people in the house again has changed our circle of friends. The exchange students bring home other great kids and we've met some really neat parents." The house is filled to overflowing with teenagers—some occasionally slipping into Norwegian.

### Define rights and privileges

Some rights come from existing, and some responsibilities come from being family. You set the standard and negotiate the details. Make sure everyone understands the difference. Physical and emotional safety, food, clothing and shelter are everyone's rights. All family members have a responsibility to respect each other's privacy, maintain their trust, help with household chores and follow the rules.

### Listen to both sides before you make up your mind

Teachers and other adults are not always right. Stand up for your grandchildren when they are right. "Battles are primarily won in the heart," explained coach Vince Lombardi, who also believed a leader "must back up the group." Many grandchildren are used to being in trouble. Having someone stand up for them is a new but critical step if trust and respect are to develop. Explain to grandchildren that life isn't equal and it isn't fair, but justice prevails. Teach them early to fight for their values but walk away from nickel-and-dime fights. Some teachers, administrators and coaches harass kids when parents or grandparents challenge them, so you too need to pick your battles.

### *Teenage driving is a privilege—not a right*

However, it can be a convenience for you. And it is a rite of passage from youth to adolescence. Here are my ground rules, which you may want to establish before you allow a driver's permit.

- Grades should be the best the student can do—for some this means A's and for others D's.

- Gas and insurance are the driver's responsibility unless the teen is involved in church, sports or other youth activities that make a job impractical.

- I pay for driver's training, turning them over to a pro as soon as they pass the written exam. They don't learn my bad habits, I don't stress out, and insurance rates are lower.

- The keys and the car are mine even if I purchase a car for their use. If they buy their own car, it doesn't leave the driveway without my approval. Sound a little harsh? Maybe, but so is death.

- Drinking or drugging means that the car and the driver are grounded. We're talking substantial lockup!

- Frequency of use, rides for friends, and mandatory chauffeuring of siblings are jointly decided.

- For safety's sake I want a pickup, or car, that will not crumple on impact, has good tires and won't win drag races.

- It's a bonus if seating is limited.

## Allowances

An allowance covering lunches, and a minimal standard of dress and school expenses is, in my opinion, a right. If you have the money, a small amount for entertainment and special purchases should be included. Some families opt to pay these expenses rather than have the youth responsible for budgeting. I disagree. It's a learning experience. It is far better to have a hungry high school freshman now than to have that freshman become a parent who spends the baby's food money. Their allowance is not dependent on doing chores such as making their beds—they make the bed because they sleep in it; they do dishes because they eat off them. They shovel sidewalks because they use them, along with the rest of the family. If youngsters need extra money, let them earn it by doing additional chores, working for neighbors or getting a job. Teach them that no honest work is without dignity.

## Curfews are flexible

If there is a legally imposed curfew for minors, respect it. I like the idea of teenagers earning later curfews by virtue of age, good grades, responsible job behavior, participation in sports or youth activities and a history of getting home on time. A fifteen-minute grace period for miscalculations, traffic or other delays seems reasonable if it is not abused. My niece and nephew can stay out until 12:30 (legal curfew is midnight); however, their own cars must be parked in the driveway by midnight. Give them selective options—but the family car is not the one to be pulled over by the police. A cell phone or money for a phone call should be part of their departure checklist. I don't like it, but in today's violent world, a car phone is more about safety than luxury. Two teenagers in our church wouldn't be alive today if a doctor hadn't had his cell phone and called Life Flight when he saw them thrown from their car as it left the road.

### Go, observe, do

Grandparent support groups offer information swaps, group therapy and family social outings. They don't appeal to everyone; nevertheless, you can meet others in situations similar to yours who are willing to nurture and assist, as well as change and grow.

### Chaperone, coach, or help at youth association, school or church functions

It's important to know who your grandchildren associate with and this is another way to meet people. During the first month when I waited with my grandson for his bus, and while being a mom helper at kindergarten, I met two daytime babysitters, another author, the mothers of three playmates for Zach, and a lady I want to interview for a magazine article. Summer evenings this year were much more pleasant as we walked, stopping to talk with neighbors who are now friends.

### *When you can't be there*

Youth clubs, before- and after-school care at elementary schools, open gyms in high schools, and park recreation programs provide fun activities and some supervision. Children need physical activity. The TV, Nintendo or computer games should be only a small portion of their day. Monitor what they watch. Cartoons, videos and computer games can be violent and openly defiant of social mores. Soaps are sleazy, and prime time shows—including sitcoms—are full of sexual innuendo, graphic groping and swearing. Music on rock stations, some videos, and many CDs are X-rated. Their content was a shock to me—and I thought I was pretty liberal. You may only be able to control what they listen to in your house, but it's a start. If you know they've watched something contrary to your belief system, create an opportunity to discuss what they saw, their feelings and their conclusions. Values are caught—as well as taught.

### *Be a grandparent, too*

Remember what it was like to go to Grandma's house? How special you felt and how specially you were treated? Stop being a parent now and then and just be a grandparent, even if it is only for a day. Overdose on junk food. Laugh at their jokes. Take them wherever you always dreamed of taking your grandchildren. Forget "please," "thank you" and brushing teeth. Let them do the planning. The only rule is this: Tell them what you are doing so that when the clock strikes midnight and you revert back to mom or dad roles, they understand.

*Indulge yourself*

When you were a first-time parent, you made sacrifices, believing your time would come when the kids were grown. As a second-time parent, you have to balance sacrificing with experiencing (not to be confused with having). Don't be a martyr with your time, emotions or money, or "you'll be tired from the heart out."[1] Seize every opportunity, dream and freedom.

*Take vacations and long weekends*

Travel as often as you can afford to, with and without your grandchildren.

*Eat chocolate in bed*

Drink espresso without remorse.

*Do miscellany*

Install the white carpet you've wanted, learn golf, buy lottery tickets, call your sister, buy a new truck, take a photography class.

*Take long baths*

Slather on the skin softener.

*Trade massages*

With your spouse or a friend.

*Watch your habits*

"We can only go where our habits take us. Your brain doesn't care which habits it reinforces—good habits feel just as natural and comfortable as bad habits."[2] Life is not traditional for either you or your grandchild, so let it be memorable.

*Relax*

The youngest siblings in a large family are almost always raised in a less structured and more casual manner. They do very well, thank you, and so will your grandchild.

Creatively avoid or enthusiastically enjoy!

———•———

Dear Zach,

I feel old. "Mom helped" at school for the end-of-year field day. Rained—but what the heck. Still a little sore from my gall bladder surgery three weeks ago (which my psychic says is from repressed anger at your mom—could be right—someday I'm going to tell her how angry I am). We ran (okay, so I walked) the track, stole the beanbags and scurried back and forth under the parachute before we were rained out. A few more hours and we're off to T-ball practice. Sometimes I wonder if I'll ever have a life? Going to ask Tomas (babysitter) if he'd be interested in teaching you to ride your bike. I just can't run fast enough or long enough to get you going. I think you're the last in your kindergarten class to learn. Better hurry, Zach. Guys have to have wheels.

Wish you were napping so I could too,

Grandma

# Chapter Six

# Attitude Is Everything, or Rather, a Positive Attitude Is Everything

*It takes a long time to become young.*
—Pablo Picasso

We all want to be proud of those we love; this is especially important to our grandchildren. Hearing "Your grandma (or grandpa) is cool" makes them feel special in a good way. Having friends approve of *you* boosts *their* self-esteem and helps dissipate guilt, anger and hurt. Many kids are ashamed of their mom or dad, and ashamed of those feelings. They carry a triple burden if we embarrass them. Being cool isn't about money, social status, or material things. It's a meshing of your mind, your soul, and your external shell.

You can be cool sitting
in a wheelchair.
On a ski lift.
At the kitchen table helping with homework.

You can be cool by being different,
yet understanding their need to be the same.

You listen.
You care.
You cry.

You understand education is living, not the ritual of
sitting in a classroom.

You praise them.
You hug them.
You say no and stick to it.

You never wear grandpa slippers to their basketball
game or your short skirt when their boyfriends visit.

They experiment. They grow. They challenge.
They try.
They love. They rebel. They conquer. They cry.
They procreate.
Dreams never die.

# Honing In on the Aging Edge

### Don't waste time sniveling

My mom says, "Life is not for sissies." Change what
you can, adapt to what you can't, face every day with enthu-
siasm and energy. One grandpa told me, "I was ugly to be
around. I was mean. I was grouchy. I pleaded with God,
then I begged, finally I tried to bargain. I'd just lost my wife
and I thought I didn't need anything more to deal with in my
life. I was wrong. Sure, I'm seventy now and I'll be eighty-

three when Nate's a senior so I probably won't chaperone the prom, but look at Walter Matthau. He's still making movies at seventy-eight. Or Neil Armstrong, who's going back to the moon. I'll be there for my grandson. He'll be here for me."

*Play on a kid's level but at your own pace*

Get down on the floor, out to the park, under a car, or to any one of the thousands of places you probably haven't seen for awhile. Be adventurous. Experiment together with makeup. Rent a snowboard. Be a counselor at church camp. Learn to skate. I took up ice skating when I was forty-nine (no tens for speed or technique, but it's fun and good exercise). Zach and I cruise the neighborhood on our bikes—he with his training wheels and me with my knee brace. Today, I wait. Tomorrow, he will. When you get tired, stop. Being there counts. Being good at the activity is a bonus.

*Learn*

Read. Take classes. Join support groups. Watch a documentary. Surf the Net. Try your grandchild's homework!

*Listen*

Stop thinking you have to have an answer. When you don't know, say so. When people need to vent, let them. Kids don't always want advice. They need to learn to solve problems, not mindlessly follow orders.

*Laugh*

"Older people have a responsibility to teach and remind younger ones that life should be fun. If older people walk around complaining about this disease or that ungrateful child, everybody under sixty is bound to believe that life is a bummer, and that it only gets worse day by day. Keeping a good attitude is really a matter of discipline, and people are responsible for having their outlook on life as positive as it can be."[1] A sense of humor is a gift everyone can share.

## Surround Sound and Other Home Improvements

Pick upbeat friends. Stop listening to the news. Acknowledge every act of kindness and support. Celebrate something every day.

Give verbal hugs every day: "I love you." "You are the best." "Could you teach me how?" "I appreciate it." Be positively honest. Do the same for yourself: "I'm proud of the weight I lost." "I did good." "I can do it." Positives in, positives out.

"Grammy, you seem so happy. What's the matter?" asked Margaret's elfin eleven-year-old, who someday wants to be an actress or model.

"Macy goes in and feeds on your psyche. Never think of her as a victim," her grandmother was told by a psychic.

"The universe picks up everything we think and feel so I send her messages of love and caring while feeding her creative soul with acting classes, gymnastics, and voice lessons," Margaret told me.

Colors of the Wind
You smell the wind of roses and fresh-cut sawdust.
You feel the wind as you sit under an apple tree
reading your favorite book.
You hear the wind blowing softly against your face
and it feels so good as you sit under that hot sun.
You taste the wind between your lips.
But do you see the colors of the wind?

To my grandma, Margaret Cramer
I love you
By Macy Margaret Langly*

## Hugs and kisses

Physical hugs, kisses and other appropriate contact are as necessary as water and sunshine. Hold a two-year-old on your lap, massage your granddaughter's neck, pat your grandson on the back. Show your emotions. Anger, tears, joy are real and should be shared.

Limit yourself to ten no's per day. If the no isn't because of health, safety or values, give your grandkids a chance to score a yes. Are there alternatives? How about "I don't have the money, but I'll pay $40 if you pay the rest." Do you need information? Ask questions. Never assume. "'Persuade me'" is a great tactic. "Persuade me why I should..." Reword your answer. "You can go as soon as you mow the lawn." Respond later. "Give me a minute (an hour, a day)." You buy time and communicate your willingness to seriously consider their request. It is especially helpful when it is a serious issue, when you have

---

*Real names. My special thanks to Margaret Cramer for letting me share Macy's poem.

mixed feelings, or when you need information from other sources.

It is counterproductive to stand firm on "no" just because you spoke in haste, but on the other hand, don't continually change your mind, giving mixed signals. "No" to yourself should be a last resort. Maybe you can't "Just Do It," but with a little ingenuity you probably "Can Do Something."

### Escape
Buy headsets for CD players and radios, for you or for them—doesn't matter. Block out what you don't want to hear. Make your bedroom off limits. Don't be afraid of saying, "You need to go to bed, or play in your room, because I need time."

### Encourage friends to come over
Theirs, so you don't have to be the playmate, and yours, so you can be the playmate.

## Clothes or Fig Leaves—Your Choice

When you are fifty or sixty you can't look twenty, and you look stupid if you try.

However, wearing "in" colors and bits and pieces of current fads keeps you looking and feeling young.

### Shoes modernize
If you've found a heel height that works, don't change. Instead, round the toe, fatten the heel or try a funky color. Buy tennis shoes with support and style. My grandson often gets the shoes off my shelf that he thinks I should wear—who says kids don't notice?

### Ditch the classic purse

Shop at T. J. Maxx, Ross, or other youth-targeted outlet stores to pick up cheap and totally "with it" purses for wrestling matches, school conferences or pizza.

### Keep favorites

Add a new top with old slacks or vice versa. When fleece is in, wear it. When polyester is out, recycle it. Often it's as easy as rolling up or down the sleeves of your shirt, taking off your socks with loafers or changing a hemline. Little kids love anything with a cartoon figure or holiday motif, whether you are parent helping or cleaning house.

### Color your hair

Our society has a mindset that gray is old. You and I are not going to change it. If you are lucky enough to have white hair, then be a stunning silver blond and flaunt it! Fellows, shave off the moustache or beard when white appears.

### Put on makeup every day

Twice a year stop by the cosmetic counter and have a free makeover. Update colors and techniques.

### Work out

Go to a health club, walk the mall, climb stairs at home. Whatever. Stay in shape to reduce stress and increase energy. It keeps you alive and living.

### Be flexible

See yourself through your grandchild's eyes. Be flexible with the small stuff.

———•———

Dear Zach,

Bobby said to you today, "I love your grandma very much," and you responded, "She's beautiful." You're only five but I hope when you are ten, fifteen and fifty you'll feel the same. I know I think you are—even after another marathon of trying to get you to sleep. The doctors put you on Clonidine but tonight, like so many nights, you jumped on the bed and ran through the house so I couldn't catch you. Then when I said I needed to calm down and went outside, you locked the doors and I had no key! Good lesson for me. It seems like the busier the day—the longer it takes you to calm down. I rubbed your back for an hour and finally you gave in and slept. It's okay. We had so much fun today. Kaitlin (your first crush) went with us for ice cream and you two sat at the kids table in the corner eating the frozen clown faces. I saw the man you will become, but just for a flash—before reality had me back mopping up chocolate faces!
Thanks for memories,

Love,
Grandma

# Chapter Seven

# Reach Me, Teach Me—
# Hidden Handicaps

*Barely avoiding drowning is not*
*considered successful swimming.*
—A. Dean Byrd and Mark D. Chamberlain
*Willpower Is Not Enough*

You can call them challenging. You can call them difficult. You can call them hyper, depressed, withdrawn, aggressive, battered, abused, neglected, or dysfunctional. There are hundreds of labels and millions of kids. Kids with hidden handicaps and emotional injuries. People see the behavior, not its causes. There's no giant Band-Aid, no temporary cast or permanent wheelchair to invoke compassion and understanding for children with fetal alcohol syndrome, attachment disorders, post-traumatic stress, and other mental-health maladies.

Pendulums swing and experts change their minds, but basically we are all products of genetics, the skills and deficiencies of our parents, our life experiences and our personal choices. Babies are born with personality traits or tendencies as well as physical attributes and defects, but these characteristics are nurtured, tolerated, controlled or changed by everything and everyone who touches their life. As surrogate parents, we must be a buffer for our grandchildren yet get them the help they need. We need to educate ourselves and others. We need to coach, counsel, console and motivate our grandsons and granddaughters. Most of all, we must be heart-over-head crazy in love with them—and show it.

# Brain Disorders and Behavior Problems

Disorders may result directly or indirectly from parental abuse of alcohol and drugs, genetics, or trauma. Following is a small guide to problem behaviors and symptoms, as well as parenting approaches, techniques for day-to-day use and relevant insight.

### *Admit you need help*
Talk to psychiatrists (who are physicians), psychologists, psychotherapists, school counselors or caseworkers. When a grandchild wheezes, wets the bed as a teenager, or squints, you see a doctor. Nothing is different about seeking relief from symptoms of abnormal behavior.

### *Accept the diagnosis and treatment*
However, don't hesitate to seek a second opinion. Medication can control abnormal behavior just as it controls diabetes or high blood pressure. Ask about side effects and alternatives. Uninformed family, friends, teachers or school administrators may attach a stigma to brain disorders and treatment. That is their problem, not yours. But to prevent

unsolicited and inappropriate reactions and advice, consider limiting the people you tell. Ask your mental health provider for help if you encounter negativity at school.

### Learn everything you can

Modify expectations but don't accept unnecessary limitations. "Do your best. I don't want you perfect" is good advice for any child. "My grandchild will be given the opportunity to try" should be your battle cry (and you will have battles) at school and elsewhere.

### Recognize that parenting will be difficult

You must create structures and boundaries to ensure calmness for yourself, commitment to your goals and continuity within your community. Develop a support team for yourself and take time off. Talking with others who have similar problems helps tremendously. They listen and share experiences.

### Fetal Alcohol Syndrome (FAS)

FAS results from alcohol abuse by the mother or father at conception and by the mother during pregnancy. "FAS is the No. 1 known cause of mental retardation in the United States...each year over 40,000 American children are born with defects because their mother drank alcohol when pregnant."[1] Its physical characteristics are identifiable but do not seem startlingly abnormal to the untrained observer—for example, short stature, a flat midface, thin lips, and heart or dental problems. Behaviors can include over-talkativeness, immaturity, a short attention span, attention-seeking and poor short-term memory. Your grandchild may have normal intelligence or lifelong learning disabilities or mental retardation. Parenting and educating the FAS child requires simple instructions limited to a single task, low environmental stimulation or distraction, written reminders and lots of repetition. Rely on structure, not control. Transition activities by forewarning ("Bedtime after this program!"), restatement ("Bedtime, the program is over!") and action ("I'm turning off TV, it's bedtime!"). Adjust your expectations to the child's developmental age. Call the National Council on Alcoholism and Drug Dependence Helpline at 1-800-622-2255 for information and local referral numbers.

### Attention disorders

These include Attention Deficit Disorder (ADD), Attention Deficit Hyperactivity Disorder (ADHD) and a combination of the two. Grandchildren with these disorders don't misbehave solely because of choice, diet or parenting deficiencies. They take in, process, and respond to information differently than others.

## ADD

Attention Deficit Disorder children are impulsive, not hyperactive. They get frustrated easily, lack social awareness, have difficulty following instructions, are easily distracted, and are often messy as they are "too impatient to clean up the debris from their last activity."[2] School can be difficult for them. They function best in small classes with short periods and multiple instruction methods, such as verbal directions and visual demonstration. At home, establish routines. Keep their belongings in the same place so they can be easily found. Write their appointments in a pocket-sized Daytimer. Place paper or whiteboards by phones and insist that your grandchild write down messages.

Ritalin or other drugs may be prescribed. Alternative therapies include homeopathic and herbal remedies, vitamin and nutritional supplements, and EEG neurofeedback.[3]

## ADHD

Attention Deficit Hyperactivity Disorder is believed to be a neurological condition caused by heredity, medical problems, or prenatal exposure to drugs and alcohol. The result is difficulty with attention, concentration, impulsiveness and self-control.[4] Kids are hyperactive and often in trouble because of their disruptive behavior. Frequently they do not get along with peers. It is "the most common of all the childhood psychiatric illnesses...some estimates put it as high as 9 percent. The overwhelming majority of kids with ADHD are boys."[5] Activities such as TV or video games that capture their interest can hold their attention for extended periods. It is important to stop unacceptable behavior at the time it occurs. Rules and structure are critical for their well being. They are high-energy, creative and hardworking. Counseling helps them develop social skills. Praise raises their self esteem. Again, Ritalin may be prescribed.

## ADD/ADHD

This disorder is a combination of hyperactivity and inattention. Keep a caregiver's diary. Note the child's activity, behavior and reaction to your attempts to modify or control his behavior for one week before an appointment with the child's psychotherapist. Have teachers and respite caretakers do the same so you can give the therapist a broad picture. Their treatments will vary but they are based on testing and observation.

Ask your doctor about occasionally removing children from medicines that may inhibit growth. Ask educators about special education school programs and the Individuals with Disabilities Education Act. Ask your accountant about tax exemptions.

## CHADD

Children and Adults with Attention Deficit Disorder is an international organization with many local support groups. It provides a valuable service for caregivers. Look in your phone book or call the headquarters in Florida at (305) 587-3700.

## Attachment disorder

This disorder may be defined as a lack of "the inner security that makes it possible for a child to pay attention also gives the child the capacity to be warm, trusting, and intimate, both with adults and with peers. Normally, we see this ability reaching an early crescendo between four and six months."[6]

Some people are born unattached. Others detach in early infancy if they are not fed when hungry, changed when wet, or held when they cry by their primary caregiver (traditionally their mother). Infants learn not to trust, and they develop "a strategy for dealing with the mother's unavailability or inconsistency."[7] As they grow they continue to cope by using inappropriate behaviors.

Symptoms can include lack of eye contact, indiscriminate affection toward strangers, superficial charm, clingy and demanding behavior, incessant talking, or cruelty to animals, self and others; recklessness with material things; or accident-prone and self-destructive behavior.[8] Parenting needs to be as physically nurturing as is appropriate and allowed by your grandchild—some unattached children reject touch. Attachment to you may develop, or it may not. Your behavior needs to be consistent and supportive in either case. Do what you say you are going to do, when you say you are going to do it—including giving consequences for misbehavior. Disapprove of unacceptable behavior, not of the child. Keep your praise simple. Expressing anger is counterproductive. It can backfire, as they will emulate and escalate the behavior. Unattached children tend to be angry or depressed anyway, so counseling is strongly recommended.

### Post-traumatic Stress Disorder (PTSD)

Many of our grandkids have seen or experienced life-threatening or serious life-altering events, such as physical or sexual abuse, neglect, abandonment or death. If these events changed their behavior, they may have PTSD. Children with PTSD see adults as dangerous, uncaring or threatening. Symptoms encompass difficulty falling or staying asleep, recurring nightmares, irritation, anger, lack of concentration, hypervigilance and fight-or-flee responses.[9] "Most children from chaotic backgrounds have learned to take care of themselves. They have not allowed themselves to be comforted or nurtured because they don't know how."[10] You must remain calm, physically nurturing, consistent and in control. Psychotherapy by trauma experts is critical. Your support is vital to their successful treatment.

The normal stages of physical, emotional and mental growth compound all the difficulties of these disorders. Your challenge is to discern whether behaviors are developmental (age-appropriate) and corresponding to society's behavioral norms, or disordered (hidden-handicapped) and then to react appropriately. Sharri Biggs, a marriage, family and child counselor who works with abused and neglected teenagers in California, recommends the Parenting Your Teen class offered by Kaiser Permanente. There are parenting classes for all age groups in every community. Ask your caseworker for recommendations, call a local hospital, or look in the Yellow Pages. Sharri Biggs hears from many adolescents that they are worried because of their grandparents' age. They worry about your dying and what will happen to them. They resent age-related physical limitations. For example, if you are unable to walk and shop the mall for extended periods, or if they have to shout when talking to you, they are disturbed. They want you to participate in their youthfully exuberant activities, even as a spectator, rather than play bingo or engage in other sedentary pastimes. Taking steps to find out what is normal and what is unique, and then discovering how other grandparents handle similar experiences, can bring you and your grandchild immense relief, hope and understanding.

—•—

Dear Zach,

    Yesterday I threatened to call the police. I had to. You were like a caged little animal running up and down the sidewalk in front of the Fred Meyer store. You wouldn't come when called and darted when I moved in your direction. Finally, I went to the car and Bobby tried—but still you wouldn't come. People were staring and I was so afraid you'd run in front of a car. I didn't know what else to do. You were mad because I said we were having hamburgers, not something from the deli. Dr. Chris (your counselor) told you today that for 21 days (and 21 consecutive days every time something like this happens) you must hold my hand or be within an arm's length if we go anywhere. I have to keep you safe. Sometimes I feel overwhelmed—so I eat, and I've already gained ten pounds, which I hate. Living with you is like living with a time bomb. I never know what will set off your temper and if you will yell, jump on the furniture, run, break another chair (or computer screen) or acquiesce with a minimum of negotiating (you're a master at it). What happens to you? I understand intellectually, but sometimes at the end of a long day or a tough week—I have to ask.

For better or worse—

Love,
Grandma

# Chapter Eight

# Normal Growing Pains

<hr/>

*Did nothing in particular, and did it very well.*
—W. S. Gilbert

"Rose-colored glasses are never made in bifocals."[1]
You can't be a grandma or grandpa and not know that kids
are like roses—beauty surrounded by thorns. If you want
blue ribbons, you put up with the manure. This chapter
expands on a few subjects discussed briefly elsewhere and
glosses over others that have been dissected and analyzed.

## Television

Kids are addicted to it. The average American
household has the television on seven hours a day.[2] That's
longer than kids are in school! It's the single biggest
influence on the way children think and their values.
According to the American Medical Association, boys and
girls see "8,000 murders and 100,000 acts of violence
before graduating from elementary school."[3] TV life is a life

of sex, false reality and violence. The news is depressing and sensationalized; sitcoms are disrespectful and titillating; cartoons are savage or fantasy, and commercials make up at least one-sixth of programming. You don't hire babysitters who expose your grandchildren to these influences—why permit television to do so? You need to set limits on time and subject matter. Follow up with discussions of what you saw (including news reports), how victims might feel, what you liked, what was bad and why. If you won't let your grandchild say it, do it, or view it in real life—turn it off. There's a whole world waiting to be experienced firsthand—chores, schoolwork, sports, drama, art projects—that cannot be experienced by surfing the polluted airwaves.

### Family mealtime

We live in a hectic world with conflicting schedules. However, eating together (without TV!) is important. A Cincinnati study found that teenagers who ate with their family five times a week, compared to three times a week, got along better with peers, did better in school and were less likely to be depressed or use drugs.[4] Bonding, building social skills, showing courtesy for the chef and respect for each other, sharing problems and triumphs, and responsibility for meal chores are all important aspects of dining together.

### Dress codes

You, not the school, should set limits for what is acceptable and unacceptable. Start with clean and neat. Purple hair, ponytails for boys and shaved heads for girls are ugly but not damaging. Tattoos are permanent and should not be permitted until after high school. Clothing that is suggestive—that exposes or lets private parts of the anatomy hang out—is vulgar. If kids don't respect themselves—who will? Earrings and body jewelry can be problematic. Set guidelines for the number and anatomical locations of piercings, as well as the age at which piercing is permissible, and the size of the jewelry. Jewelry for boys, like anything else, works in moderation. Developing taste and values while learning to make choices and accept boundaries—that's what growing up is all about.

### Hormones

Hormones are ugly when activated in juvenile bodies. There is no experience or emotional control to counteract their impact. Puberty should be abolished, no doubt about it. Teenagers' emotions change faster than a baby's temperature. They go to bed in tears and you spend the night sleepless. They wake up happy and you're frazzled. Two rules become increasingly important: (1) No friends in the house when you aren't there, and (2) No friends of the opposite sex in bedrooms. Period—end of story. You must talk about sex and diseases, sex and babies, sex and love, sex and responsibility. They know about it—most have been impacted since birth by irresponsible parents. But they need reminding in a factual, loving way, without reference to their parents, unless they initiate it, or they will become doubly defensive.

### Drugs and alcohol

"Not my child." Those are the three words that get a parent, or grandparent, into the most trouble when it comes to drugs and alcohol. They keep you from watching for changed or strange behavior, they keep you from asking questions and finding help, and they offer you false hope.[5]

No one is immune. Your grandkids may have inherited genetic factors that increase the likelihood of drug or alcohol addiction.

I've spoken with grandparents and other relatives who raised grandchildren for many years, who watched with despair as the children went back onto the streets as users.

Stormy is a babe. She lost a lot of weight and has a knockout figure but she still sees herself as fat. She and her brother lived with their Aunt Lydia and Uncle John, not their mother, for the past ten years, but the trauma of hearing that their mother died in jail last Halloween pushed Stormy over the edge, She bolted before finishing her junior year in high school. She was seen in a nearby city. It was almost two months later when I talked with her legal guardian, her aunt, who said, "They learned survival skills rather than relationship skills during the first seven or eight years of their life, as well as lying, deceit and sneakiness. They face typical teenage problems without respect for their parents or trying not to disappoint their parents, so there is little control." Her brother is a year older and a senior in high school. He calls her a "dumb s---," but I heard a few months later that he followed in her footsteps. Life on the street isn't scary when you've been there before—especially when you survive.

### Behavior change

If a behavior change lasts more than several days, investigate and act. "Zero tolerance for drugs in my home—by yourself or with friends" should be the rule. If you find drugs or evidence of usage you may need to do random drug searches and even testing. Privacy should always be respected unless it is abused. By junior high, all students know they can buy anything they want for a price—cigarettes, drugs or alcohol. You have to make it easy for them to say no. You have to tell them it is never, never okay and back up your words with appropriate education and action. You need to realize that if they are using, it takes more than willpower to overcome addictions. It takes help. Involve the school, counselors, family and your friends.

### The myth of the perfect child, the grateful child

Grandchildren aren't perfect, they make mistakes. Let them. Let them suffer the consequences—don't rush to the rescue. We can't expect great choices if they never get to practice. Let them wear pink socks with brown skirts, fall off skateboards wearing shorts, miss a birthday party because they spent their allowance, or not play in a tournament because they experimented with alcohol. While we're on that subject, if your grandchildren have a party or supply alcohol to minors you are liable. It's hard to do, but call the other parents, even if they don't thank you for it. This is "rough love." Rough love means taking action that may feel uncomfortable or awkward. "Tough love" means taking action with regard to issues or events that are severe or life-threatening. For example, tough love is refusing to post bail for a son arrested during gang violence, or kicking your daughter out of the house for continued drug use (because of her younger siblings), or calling the police when your grandchild is being abused by either parent.

### Don't expect gratitude

At best, it will be fleeting. Do expect, in times of anger and stress, statements such as "I want to live with my mommy or daddy," or "You're mean," or "Everyone else can do it!" You need a tough skin to be a parent and an even tougher one to be a parenting grandma or grandpa.

### Messy rooms and clean clothes

Teach young children and visiting playmates to clean up after themselves. Prepare to nag during the preteen years. After that, you'll have to decide if it's worth the battle or if you just want to close their bedroom door. When strange odors escape or mold grows, it's probably time for enforced solitary confinement until they muck out the mess. Children should be responsible for doing their own laundry from age six or seven. Help at first, but slowly turn over total responsibility to them. The wives of your grandsons will love you and your granddaughters also need to know.

### "Sack rats"

Hard to get them out of bed in the morning? Teach kids responsibility for their own lives. Get them an alarm clock. Help them organize their clothes, backpack, or whatever the night before and then stand back. With my grandson, I also set a kitchen timer that he carried from room to room so he could pace himself before he could tell time. If they are too young to walk to school if they miss the bus, put a jacket over their pajamas and carry them to the bus stop. Give them clothes to pull over pajamas for the first offense. When they are older, let them walk to school or take city transportation. If they have a car, take the keys.

### Kids need boundaries

They also need to test limits. When you establish expectations and enforce consequences in one area of their life it flows over to other areas and impacts future choices. They don't have to push on important issues because they know they will pay the penalty. This doesn't mean that they won't ever test or succumb to peer pressure; but if each time they do, you follow up with fair, lovingly applied discipline based on natural consequences, the learning develops.

Cindy, a crisis counselor in a large suburban school by day, moonlights for the Justice Department at night, working at the juvenile detention center to help pay the bills. Tiny-boned and petite, she's a divorced mom who listens intently to the students she counsels, and her own teenage son and daughter, because she truly and deeply cares. She tries to make contact with students who need her help, but "they have to want to participate or it won't work." Violence prevention, conflict resolution, anger management and self-esteem are talked about at student assemblies. "If one person is there for them, they have a chance—it doesn't matter if they live with a grandparent, an aunt or a significant other. If they get unconditional love they will be all right. It's those who don't have anybody—whose parents are in denial—who won't make it." Not surprisingly, most prisons offer the same type of classes. Minnesota warden Lynn Dingle added the same caveats—voluntary participation and family support are necessary for change.

### Positives and praise

Everyone does more right things every day than wrong. Yet most people, including kids, hear about the negatives. Look for good behavior and praise it immediately; as self-respect grows, so will positive behavior. Tell them in private and tell them in public. Hug them, kiss them, cuddle them, put your arm around their shoulders. It's not enough to love your grandchild. They have to hear it, see it and feel it.

## *Defiance and mistakes*

Don't shout, don't hit, and forget perfection. Grandparents know this already—most of the time. Try one-minute reprimands.[6] Do it in a timely manner when you two are alone. Tell them what they did wrong and how you feel about it, and pause for a few seconds. Remind them they are good but you can't condone their actions. Give them a loving hug or other appropriate touch and let it go. Talk about it later if your grandchild brings it up.[7] Understand your grandchild's feelings and empathize. Together, brainstorm alternatives they can try next time.

Consequences should be appropriate and slightly exaggerated. If they kick the wall, have them remove the scuff mark and clean the rest of the hallway. If they bite the child next door, go with them while they apologize to the boy or girl and their parent. If they left without telling you where they were going, ground them and give them extra chores.

If the infraction is minor, overlook it. If something happens between peers, let them work it out. If they mutter something under their breath and you've already dealt with more pressing issues, pretend you didn't hear it. If teachers complain about inappropriate behavior on a day your grandchild had a major fight with his best friend (or worst enemy, or his parent or you) ask the teacher to deal with it and explain that it was a bad day. No further explanation is necessary. Ask them to call if things don't improve.

## *Work is good*

Don't give kids everything they want. If something is important to them, they will find ways to earn it. Teach them to be selective and to evaluate worth in terms of quality, longevity of interest, price-to-self-esteem and price relative to other desires. Ask parents to not to be a "Disneyland" daddy or mommy. Suggest they buy practical presents sometimes, and occasionally oversee homework rather than go to the movies. The most important things you give your grandchildren are not things at all. There are books to read, experts to ask, and neighbors to talk to if you want to make sure that the behaviors you see really fall under the "terrible twos" or "the need to be independent teenagers" and are not abnormal. Don't overprotect or overreact. Don't let your grandchild's early years make you paranoid or send you into a panic. You've been there before, done that before, and did it very well.

— • —

Dear Zach,

When you were three and woke up with an erection it was "Oh no! It's out!" At six it's "Ain't that funky now?" from a nursery rhyme rap song you like. What will the future bring? I may not like everything you do—but I'll always love you (same thing I said to your mom when she was growing up!). I've told your counselor that sometimes I have a hard time knowing what behaviors are personality, what is typical for your age (you forget over the years), and what has been brought on by your past. Today I introduced the Chore List. You are so advanced you can read it but so typical that you don't want to do it! Bribery—ten smiley faces and we're off to the movies. Don't grow up, Zach. I need you to keep

me young—I've forgotten so much and I'm learning
even more.

Hugs, hugs, and hugs,
Grandma

# Chapter Nine

# Practically Speaking

*Just because things have changed
doesn't mean that anything is different.*
—Don I. Dickinson

Whether grandchildren are tots, teens or in-between, raising grandchildren raises questions. "The uncreative mind can spot the wrong answer, but it takes a creative mind to spot the wrong question."[1] With a twenty-one-year gap between my daughter and grandson, I find myself continually questioning things I thought I knew. Drugs, alcohol and sexual permissiveness create questions that "You never knew, you never knew."[2] Laws, government policy, and school practices vary by state, locality and circumstances, so information must be continually reverified.

### Social Security
Grandchildren must have Social Security numbers in order to be claimed as dependents on your taxes, receive

public assistance, open bank accounts, or get jobs. There is no cost for new or duplicate cards. The 800 number and local addresses can be found in the government section of most telephone directories under United States Government: Social Security.

## Birth certificates

Original or certified copies of birth certificates are required for school registration, health insurance enrollment, drivers' license applications, participation in youth athletic programs, employment, and Social Security benefits (assuming parents are deceased or disabled). Birth and adoption records are maintained by the state. Copies can be ordered for a fee, in person, by phone, fax or mail; same-day or next-day service may cost extra and some agencies require money orders, cash or credit cards (no checks). Addresses and phone numbers are in the government section of phone directories under State Offices: Health Department, birth/death certificates, or Vital Records.

## Immunization

Immunizations against diseases such as polio, diphtheria, measles, mumps, hepatitis and chicken pox are required for children in public and private schools, including preschool, unless you request a religious exemption. Keep a record of dates and shots because you will need the information if they change schools, participate in sports or go to summer camp. County health departments frequently have free or reduced-fee clinics.

## School records

Many schools will not enroll students without prior transcripts, so come prepared. You should periodically review your grandchild's official file. Requests need to be in writing and advance notice given. "Inaccurate public school records may prejudice teachers and school officials against your child as he moves up through the grades and may reduce his chances of getting into the college of his choice. Under the Family Educational Rights and Privacy Act you can lawfully inspect your child's public school records and request correction of inaccurate entries. Corrections should be limited to matters other than grades: a grade will not be changed unless it was incorrectly recorded."[3] If the school refuses, or does not respond within forty-five days, you may request a hearing. Contact your state superintendent of education or the Family Educational Rights and Privacy Act Office in Washington, D.C.

# School and Social Activities

### *Prepare for sticker shock*
Many high schools, at least in Oregon, require $150 per activity for student participation. This does not include choir robes, rally squad uniforms, off-season training clinics, Gatorade, etc. For first-grade extra activities, I paid $65 for Little League plus $150 for uniform, cleats, ball, bat and glove; soccer cost $35 plus $20 in lieu of fund-raising, and I supplied ball, cleats, shin guards, water bottles, etc. Needless to say, team snacks, pictures, trophies and parties are always extra. Laptop computers are *de rigueur* in college, as is a hookup to schools' Intranet and phones. High-tech equals high-cost.

### *AIDS, STDs, birth control and pregnancy*
Tests for pregnancy or sexually transmitted diseases, including AIDS, can be done by physicians, clinics, nurse

practitioners, and the county health department. Most insurance policies cover at least some of the cost although prior approval is often required.

"Women with HIV can pass the virus to their newborns during pregnancy, childbirth, and through breast feeding."[4] Young children should be tested if they have been sexually abused (infected persons may not know or disclose their disease), or if there is reason to believe they were infected by contaminated needles. State laws vary in requiring parental or guardian consent for testing of sexually active minors or drug users. Some states have partner notification laws so positive test results may be handled confidentially but not anonymously. Most hotlines will mail you brochures that are very helpful. Generally, if someone does not test HIV positive within six months of contact he will not get the disease.[5] Many facilities will only give results in person and offer immediate counseling for those who test positive. There are support groups, special day care centers, respite care providers and other help available if you are raising HIV- or AIDS-infected grandchildren. Look in the Yellow Pages under Aids Information and Treatment. Two national hotlines I found especially helpful were the AIDS National Hotline (1-800-342-2437 or 1-800-344-7432 for Spanish) and the Teen AIDS Hotline (1-800-440-8336).

*Prevention of AIDS, sexually transmitted diseases (STDs) and unwanted pregnancies requires fully informed and responsible sex partners*

This means you need to educate your grandchildren in precautionary measures. Educate yourself first. Begin discussions with your grandchildren when they are young. They must always feel they can ask you questions about sex or talk to you if they are in trouble. Listen carefully and respond rationally. Using a condom is greater than 10,000 times more effective than not using one, according to Ronald Carey on the Siecus Internet Page, "The Truth About *Latex* Condoms." *Latex* (italicized for emphasis) condoms substantially reduce the risk of getting HIV or STDs. Spermicides may offer extra protection when using a condom but they cannot replace condoms. Lubricants help keep condoms from breaking during anal sex; however, use only water-based ones, such as K-Y brand—not oil-based such as Vaseline, which can destroy the latex. Store condoms in cool dry places—not in wallets or glove boxes where they can be damaged by heat. "You can't get HIV or AIDS from someone by kissing, although deep kissing may be risky. Infected body fluids can pass through small cuts and sores in the mouth," warns the American Social Health Association. Abstinence is the only birth control method that provides 100 percent protection from sexually trans-mitted diseases.

### Birth control information, pills and other preventative aids

These are available for sexually active teenagers. Look under Birth Control in the Yellow Pages or call your doctor, nurse, or the county health department. If prevention fails, pregnant girls have a right to continue their education. Contact local district offices for education options.

### Abortions and alternatives to abortion

In some states abortions can be obtained without parental or guardian consent or notification. This means you may never know if your granddaughter has had an abortion or have any access to medical records. Other states require a court hearing to determine if the girl is "mature enough to make the decision after consulting with her doctor, or if the abortion was ruled to be in her best interest."[6]

## Abortion and pregnancy counseling

Organizations that counsel against abortions and help girls during their pregnancy with housing, medical care, clothing, etc. (whether they wish to keep their babies or place them for adoption) may be found under Abortion Alternatives in the Yellow Pages. Health care providers that perform abortions or make referrals to individuals providing abortions can be found under Abortion Providers or Abortion Providers' Referral Services. I strongly recommend going with your grandchild. While working for the Yellow Pages I heard a few heart-rending and blood pressure-raising stories from parents about experiences their daughters encountered at some businesses. On the other hand, my daughter selected an adoption agency after calling an organization in the phone directory, and they were the most wonderful, caring and open people imaginable.

## Housing

The Federal Fair Housing Act strictly prohibits discrimination against families with children by any apartment complex, housing development, mobile home park, school dormitory, or any other planned community (with very few exceptions) or shelter used for residential housing. If you are threatened, evicted or denied access to housing owing to having your grandchild residing with you, contact the nearest Federal Fair Housing office which can be found in your phone book's government section under United States: Housing.

*Clothes, toys, etc.*

Shopping is normally an immediate necessity. Be sensitive to your grandchild's feelings. Children "struggle with loyalty issues vacillating between their birth parents and grandparents."[7] Discarding possessions can be threatening and make them feel disloyal. Clothes and other belongings are links to parents and reflect their own self-image and identity.

If you want inexpensive clothing and toys, go to garage sales. At thrift stores you may have to pick through stacks or go back a number of times, but if you are persistent you can find good quality at affordable prices. Many stores have reasonable prices and current styles. I like K-Mart, Target and Mervyn's for infants, toddlers and young children. T. J. Maxx, Ross, J.C. Penney, Nordstrom Rack and youth-targeted chains such as Zumiez, the Gap or the Limited specialize in trendy fashion for teenagers. Nordstrom, Elizabeth, and the Bon Marché offer chic and classic styles, albeit with higher price tags. Clothing and sports equipment resale and consignment shops differ; however, most carry brand-name merchandise in good condition at moderate prices. These stores are especially good if you have items such as ski pants, snowboards, soccer shoes or hockey pads to exchange for credit on larger sizes or upscale models. Outlet malls are okay, but unless there is a change of season or closeout of last year's styles, you can find comparable prices on sale at retail stores.

# Safety and Other Stuff

*Airbags can kill*

Children twelve years old and under are safer in the back seat of the car. Never place a rear-facing car seat in front or hold a child on your lap. Children under forty pounds should always be in a car seat; check your car owner's manual for safety belt or harness instructions.

### Home safety
Child-proof for toddlers by adding safety plugs to electrical outlets and gates at the top of stairs. Put poisons, including medicines, household cleaning, automotive and gardening products, out of reach or in locked cabinets.

### Fire alarms
Install fire alarms in or near all bedrooms. Check them at least every six months to ensure they are working. Have fire escape plans and drills.

### Emergency medical care
Authorize emergency medical care: when traveling, give a relative or friend signed and dated written permission to authorize emergency medical care. Include the legal names of your grandchild, yourself and authorized parties. Attach insurance cards, the name and phone number of your grandchild's doctor and information about how to reach you. If the state has legal custody of the child write down the caseworker's name and an emergency phone number. If the parents have custody, you and others must have their written permission for routine or emergency medical treatment.

### Helmets
Required for bicyclists and skateboarders in many states. Consider knee and elbow pads for young skaters.

### Limit backpack weight for young children
Prevents spinal damage. This is especially important if your grandchild's school does not have lockers.

*Door locks*

Install locks on your bedroom and bathroom doors for privacy. Put extra keys in a separate location for emergencies.

*Keepsakes*

Create a baby book, a scrapbook, a photo album, and save their favorite toys and clothes as well as school mementos. Keep pictures of grandkids and their parents if possible, as well as letters, gifts, or other memorabilia from their mom or dad. These may be all they will ever have besides memories.

*Easy contact*

A pager or mobile phone makes it easy for grandchildren to reach you—and vice versa.

*Computer equipment*

Computers and color printers are required by many schools for homework. Call computer teachers at high schools or sixth-grade teachers for elementary grades before you buy. It will be easier for your child if you have the same computer type, i.e., IBM- or Macintosh-compatible, and software programs similar to those used at school. Many classrooms have computers but they seldom have one for every student. If you have limited money, contact local businesses and ask to purchase outdated equipment. Resale value is low due to rapid technology improvements. Educational and recreational games are secondary benefits; their use should be monitored as carefully as television.

*Clip coupons and use discounts*

Sometimes a combination of senior and youth (or student) discounts may be cheaper than family rates. Many membership organizations such as Price-Costco, AAA and credit unions negotiate discounts for products and services from unrelated businesses. Local establishments such as pizza parlors, movie theaters and beauty salons often give student discounts with picture-I.D. school cards.

### Think about college funding

Call your tax advisor and start a college fund today; new improved tax laws were passed in 1997. It's never too early, or too late, and even small amounts grow. Other options include college prepayment and frozen-dollar plans. Write to colleges or contact the state superintendent of higher education. One of the hazards of our information age is option overload, so screen ideas with friends or acquaintances. Other parents, grandparents, and support groups are all good resources.

—●—

Dear Zach,

You're so trusting and snuggly. I always hold you when we sit and read or when Bobby comes over and we watch TV. Bobby started rubbing your back six months ago when you first came—now you're addicted and will place my hand under your shirt or pajamas and start moving it up and down. Today I took you for a blood test to see if you are HIV positive. You're scared of doctors and nurses—because of the exams after the beating, I'm sure. I'm scared of AIDS. I sat in the big chair with you on my lap and together the nurse and I got you calm enough that she could draw blood. I don't think Todd or Dylan would ever have

infected you on purpose but I'll never forgive
Brandy for exposing you. Why doesn't she have
any of the normal mothering instincts? I don't
sleep well anymore—my brain doesn't shut off like
it used to—and I'm so tired of crying. Oh well.

Goodnight my little angel,
Grandma

## Chapter Ten

# Safe Is a Good Four-Letter Word

*It takes a lot of practice to grow.*
*Let them get more practice.*
*You have to give them more time.*
> —Zach Callander, age four,
> looking at bare-root roses

"Safe" takes a bad rap. No one wants to be afraid to take chances, said Katherine Hepburn: "If you obey all the rules, you miss all the fun." Good advice, if you know which to keep and which to break. Our world is dangerous and our grandchildren are at risk. I may be street-naive but if the following doesn't scare you spitless you're either a fool, an incurable optimist or comatose.

## Child Abduction and Kidnapping

Three hundred fifty thousand children per year are taken by noncustodial parents.[1] It is illegal—an act of revenge, not love. Many children are never found. Finding and getting back those that are located can bankrupt you financially and emotionally. Parents move frequently and scare children into silence with horror stories of what will happen to them, or you, if they tell. Children don't recover. As adults, they lie, refuse to trust and can't bond. "It's my worst nightmare," a grandfather confided at a foster grand-parent support group, and a lot of heads nodded. "If Jose even goes outside to rollerblade, someone has to be there to watch. His dad has made threats and hates me enough that he would do it. He doesn't want Jose but he never thinks ahead to the consequences. I worry. I make Jose wear bright clothing so I can spot him easily. I worry when he's at school. I tell other parents and coaches to never let him leave with anyone but me. Unless I'm dead, I'll pick him up."

### Practice dialing 911 with your grandchildren
By age three they should know your address, area code and phone number.

### Tell them you care
Tell them constantly you will always love them, that you would never agree to their parent or a stranger taking them, and that you will always keep looking for them if they disappear.

### Reinforce their feelings of safety
Reassure them that you will be safe regardless of what they are told.

### Safe strangers
Roleplay identifying safe strangers such fast-food servers, gas attendants, policemen, grocery clerks or

teachers at new schools, and how to ask for help.

## Explain what "kidnapped" means

Help your grandchild practice screaming "I'm being kidnapped! Call the police!" Tell them that when they are questioned they need to use the word "judge" so people understand the severity of the problem. Have them practice saying "The judge said I need to live with Grandpa because Daddy has problems," for example.

## Pick a code word known only to you and your grandchild

Advise them never to go with their parents unless you've told them about the visit in advance. Have a designated third party they can call if you aren't available when a parent shows up unexpectedly. Roleplay frequently, testing to see if they give Aunt Betsy, Mom or best friend Joe the secret word and to ensure that you both remember the word. Tell them if it feels wrong, don't go. Explain that they can call you or the police anytime, anyplace and you will stand by them. Explain "Better embarrassed than abducted" to them. Change your code word if you ever use it.

## Out-of-state travel

Specify in the custody order that no out-of-state travel is to occur without written permission, and that police or the FBI will be involved if the decree is violated. File for a denial of passport with the Passport and Advisory Services at 111 19th St., NW, Suite 260, Washington, D.C., if you are concerned that their parents may try to leave the country. Include a copy of the court order with case number.[2]

*Listen and observe*

If the noncustodial parent parent quits his or her job, disconnect the phone or sell house or possessions— something is wrong. Call your attorney and get supervised visits only, until the parent is firmly rerooted in the community.

*Family and auto information*

Write down the parents' car license number, color, make and year. Keep names and numbers of in-laws, friends and employers.

*Regular photos*

Twice a year take a full-face photos of grandchildren and both parents and write down physical descriptions including weight, height, and color of hair. One in seven missing children is found by identification through photos.[3]

*If your grandchild is taken, call police and an experienced family-law attorney immediately*

Time is critical. They can activate national locator services and access information to help trace your grandchild—such as school, motor vehicle or telephone call records.

# Gangs

*Why gangs?*

Gangs fulfill needs resulting from latchkey loneliness, parental rejection, fear for safety of self, family or possessions, peer pressure, ethnic rivalries and drug use.

*Supervise, supervise, supervise!*

Know your grandchild's friends. Know where they are at all times. Make it a rule that you are always able reach them with one phone call. Enforce curfews. Meet parents. Insist that overnight, after-school visits and parties are chaperoned. Be selective about who is allowed in your home when you are out (if you choose to allow it). Living in your house is reason enough for them to abide by your rules.

*Support sports and school activities*

Make sure the school's coaches and activity leaders are good role models. Jobs are good for kids if they are accountable and responsible for their time and wages. A caveat: too much money attracts the wrong friends and the wrong activities.

*Discuss gangs beginning in preschool*

Talk about pain and violence. Deglamorize gangs. Champion mandatory community service in rest homes, parks, schools and places where peers can see menial work being done by juvenile offenders and gang members. Show your grandchild some community service work crews.

*Learn about gangs*

Contact schools and police to learn gang colors and dress (jackets, headbands, insignia, etc.), hand signs and other telltale indications. Get help if your grandchild is approached, minimally involved or deeply enmeshed. Be alert for changes in their friends or reluctance to talk about school or extracurricular activities.

## *Self confidence*

Promote self-confidence through martial arts, communication, and self-defense training. If they struggle academically, work together nightly, hire tutors, and talk to teachers. Low achievers get positive reinforcement from gangs. Give your grandchild all possible opportunities to achieve and to be self-confident.

## *Model saying no*

Give no reasons and no excuses. Be firm, and use humor as appropriate. Stress avoiding gang hangouts, including certain restrooms or hallways at school. Give kids the information and skill to know when to handle a problem and how, and when to ask for help.

## *Knives and guns kill*

Possession implies intent to use. Be absolutely certain they know that backing down or walking away, even when they are right, saves lives.

## *Do things together*

Say "I love you" and "You're special." Hug them and hold them. Praise them in front of others. Never let them feel they are a burden or think they are responsible for their parents' failures.

## *Join neighborhood watches*

Keep drugs, prostitution, adult bookstores and topless bars out of your community. Do not allow violent or sexually offensive movies in your home. Stand up for your values. They are the values you wish to share with your grandchild.

# Sex, Rape, and Abuse

*Safe sex isn't*

The smorgasbord of possible consequences include pregnancy, AIDS, herpes and other sexually transmitted diseases, loss of reputation, lifetime trauma, guilt and possibly death. Sex education classes and street talk aren't enough.

*Call body parts by anatomical name*

Every child needs to know that no one except a doctor has the right to touch them. Likewise, they should never be asked to inappropriately touch, hold or kiss the body parts of others. If they are, they need to be able to say no and tell others about it. They can't tell you if they are molested when they don't know the words or what is wrong for adults to do. *Not My Child!* by Jan Wagner is one of the best books I've found. There are many others to read with children. Ask at your bookstore or library for help in locating effective books.

*Saying no*

Everyone has the right to say no, whether they are a preschooler or a sexually active teenager on a date.

*Condoms*

Latex condoms can fail if they are improperly applied, or stored or used beyond the expiration date. Natural fiber condoms protect from pregnancy but not from AIDS.

*Contacts*

Establish a tree of people your grandchild can talk with if they have problems. Include yourself, other family members, teachers, church or youth leaders, etc. Tell them if they can't talk about something, to write it down and give it to you or someone they trust.

# Drugs

*Reread the section on gangs*

Most of the same information applies. Keeping your grandchildren busy and feeling loved, safe and good about themselves is the greater part of the battle.

*You and they need to talk*

Many grandchildren have experienced the freedom, as well as the pain, of living with users or using themselves. You need to talk. A lot. Living on the streets isn't terrifying to them—their parents may be there now.

*Avoid preaching*

Instead, create opportunities to discuss what they've seen, heard and felt but don't generalize, make statements without facts or label their parents as bad.

*Set an example*

Don't overindulge. Don't drink and drive. And never use illegal drugs. Minimize your use of prescription and over-the-counter medicines and recognize that smoking is an addiction. So is caffeine.

*Lethality*

The average street purity of heroin is now 40 percent, which is ten times higher than it was twenty years ago. In 1996, four thousand deaths due to heroin overdose occurred.[4]

*Recognize the symptoms of substance abuse*
Inhalants, such as glue, can cause decreased appetite, irritability, dizziness, sores around the mouth and nose, and loss of memory or concentration. Other drugs, such as cocaine or speed, produce some of the same signs including body sores, weight loss, hyperactivity, dilated pupils, excessive talking, scarred veins and rapid mood swings.

# Happy Endings

In gambling, repetition doesn't change the odds. If you flip a coin the odds are always 50-50 that tails will come up. There is a finite combination, with finite odds for any specific number combination, that can occur in a lottery. In life, repetition changes the odds. Create opportunities for the child to learn safety principles by seeing, saying and doing. The more your child knows, the better prepared he or she is to avoid or escape danger. Planning, practice and prayer—don't let your grandchild leave home without them.

——●——

Dear Zach,
Today at your little two-hour-a-day, two-week summer school "Safety Town" you learned about "stranger danger." How sad that for you, a greater danger is your dad. The district attorney warned his mom in court that if he ever took you they'd "hunt him down like a dog." Not an idle worry, ask me when you're older about his call offering to get out of your life for money. Or ask Grandpa Lowell about his conversations with

Donald. Thank God you have Grandpa Lowell and Nana who would protect you, as would I, with our lives.

I hope you're having fun this weekend with Mommy,

Love,
Grandma

# Chapter Eleven

# 101 Ways to Have
# Fun on a Budget
# (With or Without Grandkids)

---

*Don't sweat the small stuff: It's all small stuff.*
*Since it usually doesn't work to fight and it*
*usually doesn't work to flee, flow.*

—Thomas F. Crum
*The Magic of Conflict*

A good offense is your best defense. A lot of trust-building, loyalty and learning come from good times spent together. A frequent complaint heard during support groups for kids being raised by grandparents was lack of grandparents' participation in high-energy activities, according to Jeri Alcock (formerly of Network Behavioral HealthCare, Inc.).

It doesn't take much to remedy this. Swing together at the park, play catch or go swimming—and anticipate a high level of fun. Remember though, that you need balance. You need the stress reduction and relaxation you get from play time with other adults or alone time by yourself.

Money buys conveniences such as babysitting, transportation and getaways, offers Jeri. The less money you have, the more creative you need to be about activities. Here are some old and new ideas for fun and stress reduction:

- Take a hot-air balloon ride.

- Go for a walk after dark.

- Stop for a cup of coffee at a restaurant with outside tables.

- Sign up for skiing lessons through your local community college.

- Chaperone a high-school ski team and ski free.

- Window-shop at the mall.

- Buy a lottery ticket and play Things to Do When We Win.

- Browse through a secondhand bookstore.

- Take up line dancing.

- Play tic-tac-toe with sidewalk chalk.

- Chase bubbles.

- Buy a keno ticket for a friend.

- Join a seniors' soccer league.

- Jog on the beach.

- Help decorate a department store for Christmas as a money-raising project for schools.

- Stay up all night reading.

- Buy a loaf of hot bread from a bakery.

- Eat pie for breakfast.

- Fly to Reno on a cheap red-eye twenty-four-hour trip.

- Take a stuffed animal to a kids' hospital.

- Volunteer to rock drug babies.

- Refurbish old furniture.

- Paint a wall in your house an outrageously energizing color.

- Take a tour of local wineries or microbreweries.

- Have your fingernails done in a holiday motif.

- Take a weight-training class.

- Lie in the sun.

- Turn on a talk show.

- Visit an after-hours art show.

- Go to a jazz concert.

- Play Frisbee.

- Spend an afternoon going to garage sales.

- Take a wilderness-survival class.

- Be a volunteer camp counselor or cook.

- Go on a mission to another country with your church.

- Learn to rollerblade.

- Put on a fake tattoo.

- Try cold ceramics at home.

- Go to a parade.

- Take a picnic and meet a friend for lunch.

- Have a spaghetti party.

- Play jacks.

- Go swimming.

- Make a collage.

- Teach someone to whistle.

- Buy and play *The Full Monty* CD or cassette.

- Take a bubble bath.

- Have a complementary makeover at a department store.

- Mow the lawn for an elderly neighbor.

- Do twelve days of birthday for your grandchild.

- Organize a Name-the-Baby photo contest at work.

- Record a funny message on your answering machine.

- Tell someone else a joke a day for a week.

- Slip a funny slide into a business presentation.

- Play What's-in-the-Bag with grandkids.

- Go on a whitewater or canoe trip.

- Sneak popcorn into a movie theatre.

- Pack your spouse's bag and treat them to a night at a bed and breakfast.

- Read out loud.

- Treat yourself to brunch.

- Color a raw egg along with hardboiled eggs at Easter.

- Make your own gift wrap.

- Climb a tree.

- Rent a bicycle for two, or three, or four.

- Buy and go fly a kite.

- Tour a candy factory.

- Make a gift basket of auto parts for a college student.

- Have a Hawaiian potluck.

- Volunteer at a food kitchen.

- Learn to knit.

- Play a musical instrument.

- Practice blowing bubbles with your gum.

- Take a child to play on swings at a park.

- Go park with your husband, wife, or special friend.

- Wear a funny sweatshirt.

- Visit a psychic.

- Tie a ball of string to a present and wind it up stairs and down, in and out of the house.

- Buy a balloon.

- Go to a locally produced play.

- Go camping.

- Collect posters for your garage.

- Rent a convertible the first sunny weekend of the year.

- Have a champagne walk in your neighborhood.

- Find an old wooden set of Pick-up Sticks.

- Play cards.

- Buy a barking cookie jar for your dog's treats.

- Join a singles club.

- Take aerobics.

- Learn water ballet.

- Take time to enjoy the color of the roses outside your window.

- Go barefoot in the house.

- Fingerpaint.

- Take a child to story hour at a local library.

- Visit your local Saturday Market.

- Hide stuffed animals in your house and have a Spring Break Safari.

- Try to figure out the answers in *The Mensa Genius Quiz Book*.

- Plant sweet peas.

- Call a discount cruise broker and go somewhere on the spur of the moment.

- Go to the airport, have a drink, pretend you are going on a trip.

- Watch reruns of your favorite movies and look at old photos.

———•———

Dear Zach,

"It's a song, song, song about a shark, shark, shark." We just finished videotaping you singing a song from your first day at Camp Tillicum. You are so happy and that makes me glad, but I'm sad that you sat on the bus by the junior high counselor, not another child. You're the same but different, I feel, from the others on the four busloads of kids. I, too, feel different—older than the other moms and dads who stand and wait as the buses load and then unload at the end of the day. It was 101 degrees today and I worried all day, but you seem fine. Let's go buy you a spray bottle for water fights tomorrow...

Love,
Grandma

# Chapter Twelve

# Good Grief, Bad Guilt

*I used to have dreams*
*But now I have hope.*

—Judith McNaught, *Perfect*

When adult children make bad choices, it is hard to remember that they are *their* choices. You are not responsible. Their actions are not a reflection on you. You are not a bad person and probably weren't a bad parent. No one deliberately sets out to screw up her child's life. Parents do their best and then try to live with the results.

"Each human being has a story, and the traumas and betrayals are real. Each individual responds to these realities in his or her own unique way. We are not simple formulas of cause and effect."[1] Everyone and everything that touches a child has an impact—genetics, parents, friends, peers and schools. Parents have the opportunity to mitigate circumstances, alter environments and teach coping skills if genetics or fate is cruel. Life can be a bummer. We suffer when our children hurt. We mourn when they die or make dead-end choices.

# The Guilt Trip

You can't cancel the past. If you gave your children boundaries, discipline and love you fulfilled the parental contract. If you handed them too many material things, worked too many hours, clung too hard, were overly permissive or overly controlling, so what? We all had things in our childhood that caused us to say, "I'm never going to do that to my kids." We may or may not have kept our vow, but the point is—we overcame what we thought was unfair or ugly. Expectant parents are apt to say "My kids will never do that!" but seldom do you hear these words from parents of teenagers. Experience teaches, and experience humbles. All people are born with basic personalities and, like cars, some may fall apart due to neglect, accidents or abuse.

# If Only—

Single parents can't be everything to their sons or daughters and many feel guilty that they aren't. Give it up. It is true that our progeny do best with both a healthy male and female role model, but the role model can come from extended family, friends and contacts outside the home. A loveless marriage, an abusive marriage, a marriage with an unfaithful mate—how many more devastating influences there are than single parenthood.

Adoptive parents can't be everything. Working moms and dads can't be everything. Young, old, white, black,

American Indian, Catholic, Jewish, gay or straight—no one can be all things to their children. I wish with all my heart that I had stayed home instead of working. I am totally convinced that when moms started working, America started its decline.

If only I could have prevented the pain my daughter had about being adopted. If only I had never married an adult child of an alcoholic. I can't undo the pain or the past. What I can do is be thankful for the good things my ex-husband and I shared and provided. Our adopted daughter had a loving and safe home. One or both of us attended school programs, conferences and sports events. We all went camping. She and I attended church. We all had counseling. She had chores and responsibilities. I'm sorry she was an only child, sorry she didn't have a best friend, sorry we lived in the country, sorry her dad and I separated when she was a freshman in college, sorry about a lot of things.

But from experience, I know that guilt is not the answer. Only God knows what would have happened if you and I had done things differently. Move on, as painful as the journey may be. Guilt is only good if it motivates positive action. Don't excuse children from accountability. Don't let yourself become a martyr or a victim.

"Mom's seventy-two and diabetic," Dee Dee worries as she cuts her client's hair. "She skips insulin shots when her insurance doesn't pay and she never eats properly. When she's worried, her skin rash or irritable bowel flares up, but my alcoholic sister pretends nothing's wrong. Mom's taken care of my seventeen-year-old nephew, Seth, off and on since Sis got pregnant in high school, a few years after Dad died. Mom speaks Dutch, and not much English, so I always read important papers to her. She's made her grandkids her life and my sister takes advantage of it.

Occasionally, Mom tries to draw the line but she's not consistent, so then I try to step in. The whole family is dysfunctional and they expect me to fix things." Take control of your life—you are the only person you can change. If you're not in control of yourself, there isn't much hope for your children or grandchildren.

# Addictions

*There will be more rejoicing in heaven over one sinner repenting than over ninety-nine upright people who have no need of repentance.*
—Luke 15: 4-7

People who abuse drugs, including alcohol, are not rational. Logic does not work with them. They don't respond to love or natural consequences. They aren't bad; they are sick. "If at first you don't succeed, try, try again. Then quit. There's no use being a damn fool about it." This quote from W. C. Fields is out of context, I'm sure, but in my mind it applies directly to parents of drug users.

Do everything you can to prevent experimentation. Learn to recognize the signs of drug use. If your child chooses to use, don't enable the behavior. Cut off financial help; suggest counseling; pay for maybe one live-in rehabilitation program. If they don't quit drugs entirely, get them out of your house or, if they have children, get the grandkids out of their house. Sound cruel? It isn't. Parents can spend thousands of dollars trying to help children who won't change. A probation officer told me that drug rehab programs for young offenders often don't work, because users are with others who abuse. Then they form support systems. They complain about parents, school, life—

anything and everything but themselves. They have new suppliers when released. They continue to lie. They steal from you and your neighbors; they even steal from their own kids. They hock bicycles, stereos or anything of value to obtain one more hit.

# Letting Go

One grandmother said, "I told my daughter, 'I've changed the locks and don't you dare come around here looking for something to fence when I'm at work.' I told Georgio, my grandson, 'I'm not buying you any more bikes or Walkmans if you let your mom in the house when I'm not here, because she stole your last ones.' He gets really angry then and makes excuses for her because he loves her, and she tells him someone else took them. I try not to argue in front of him, but this has been going on since he was two years old—nine years ago. I'm fifty-seven. His mom is fine in front of him and then steals on her way out the door. My grandson and I live alone now. Two years ago Edward lived with me, but he was drunk a lot and I had to keep him away from Georgio." Grandparents need to get tough and *let go*. Some children's rock bottom is further down than you, or I, can possibly imagine.

Nagging self-doubt and the question "Where did we go wrong?" resurface as grandchildren suffer. There is nothing more devastating to a grandparent. Mothers, we think, should protect their young by instinct. We expect the same from fathers. We don't condone physical or sexual abuse by anyone, but somehow it seems worse when the mother does the abusing, neglecting or endangering. Anger replaces sympathy. Illusions are gone. Dreams are gone. Guilt turns to grief.

# Grief

When you lose a child to death, drugs, alcohol, disease or criminality, you must grieve. Loss of a dream is sometimes harder to come to terms with than loss of a life. There is no sign that says "The End." There is no memorial service or forced termination. Your mind says "This is it." Your heart says, "Maybe not."

Common sense is life's best antidote. You need to talk. Get counseling, join a support group, talk to family or friends and find others who have had similar experiences. What's inside has to come out. All of it—the words, the anger, the fear and the tears. I spent $35 tuition for a five-week grief release class. There, I learned how to grieve over lost hopes as well as lost children. I tapped into hidden reservoirs of anger. The suicide of a former boss, abandonment by my friends when I divorced, two failed marriages—all had to be mourned before I could move on to accept that my daughter, as I had known her, was also gone. Once you know what's making you feel bad, "Why me?" changes to "Why not me? What can I learn? How can I help others?" And then you start healing.

# Anger

Anger and resentment must be released. A widow, whose husband had not filed tax returns for two years before his death, recently asked me, "How can you be mad at someone who is dead?" The answer is easy—the same way you can be mad at a son who is in jail or a daughter who aborted or abused your grandchild. It doesn't matter if they are sitting across from you, or if they are buried in the ground or living on the streets. When you feel wronged, you have the right to be angry. You have a right to say out loud or commit to paper, "I'm angry because..."

It took me four years to tell my daughter, "I'm angry." Then I only said I was angry because she hurt Zach, angry because we can't have normal Christmases or barbecues together, angry because every ounce of my energy is used every day in raising her son. "When you come take him," I said, "I do not want to sit and visit. I need the time alone." I didn't tell her how angry I was about the fourteen thousand dollars it cost me for legal fees, bail, counseling, and repaying at least one of her debts. I didn't tell her I'm furious because Zach is fueled with anger. She listens to words and tries to correct the slightest inaccuracy. I tell her, "Listen for emotions—he's mad at you and he's trying to tell you." I didn't tell her I've lost my old friends—I don't have the time, money or the emotional energy it takes to go out, entertain or work at being a friend.

She doesn't understand how hard it is to have a six-year-old who won't go in another room unless you go with him—who crawls up on your lap or calls to you from the bathroom, the living room or the school bus dozens of times a day to say "I love you." He's really saying "I'm scared. I need you. And yes, I love you." I don't talk to her a lot because I really don't know exactly how I feel right now. Zach's counselor says, "Nowhere is it written down that you have to like your child." I defended Brandy too many times, and too many times she cut my heart to pieces. I love her, but all my efforts are focused on healing Zach—not our relationship.

For our sanity, you and I eventually need to forgive our sons and our daughters or they will control the rest of our lives. For example, "I forgive you for dying and leaving me to raise your children," and "I forgive you for stealing the ring your father gave me for our tenth anniversary. I forgive you for abusing your son. It was wrong—but I choose to forgive."

Say goodbye. Some examples are "Goodbye to my dreams of a wedding for you, my daughter," "Goodbye to family hunting trips," "Goodbye to the little boy and young adult I loved; I don't like and won't embrace his replacement," "Goodbye to our Saturday golf games, Joseph," "Goodbye to verbal abuse," and "Goodbye to teddy bears, senior proms and happily-ever-after. I'll always cherish the good memories, but I'm moving on."

Joanne Smith, a grief counselor in Portland, Oregon, and author of *How to Say Goodbye*, suggests an accompanying physical act which can be something as simple as snapping your fingers, a graveside chat, blowing out a candle, or shredding a goodbye letter. The physical act embeds the goodbye in your mind as well as your heart. Grief comes and goes. There will still be good and bad days. She says, "Feel all there is to feel, and later, remind yourself that you survived. After a while you'll do more than survive, you'll thrive. Because the other side of fear is excitement. And the other side of doing is the reward and positive feeling you seek."[2]

You need to repeat, or simultaneously work through, the process of letting go of guilt and grief if your marriage comes apart due to stress or disagreement over whether to raise grandkids. It is not uncommon. Raising grandchildren is "a "bittersweet job" stated Dr. Rosa Jones, an associate professor of social work at Florida International University, in a 1996 article in *Woman's Day* magazine. The article continued, "grandparents often find the personal costs high, including physical and marital stress, financial burdens and isolation from peers."

Be kind and gentle, firm and forgiving with yourself and your family. Consider what the Dalai Lama said: "My religion is very simple. My religion is kindness."

Guilt and grief will pass.

— • —

Dear Zach,

I spent the day at the courthouse looking up all the criminal records on your mom, Todd and Dylan. I should have done it years ago, but the hurt was too raw and the need to believe your mom too strong. I often wondered what I did wrong—but that's finally gone now. You are legally and emotionally mine, and, after all these years, I'm ready to say "I'm angry." I know I need to work through it. Your mom's in denial still and I'll call her at every turn but I won't go out of my way to hurt her. I know Ryan hates me but then he doesn't know "the rest of the story." Better that he doesn't. You deserve a mom, so I'll keep the fairytales going but she was as bad, or worse, a mother as your father (whom you hate) was a father.

Like the line out of the *Fox and Hound* movie that we've watched so many times together—"you poor little child."

I won't let your mother ruin what's left of my life—or yours.

Hugs and kisses,
Grandma

# Chapter Thirteen

# Tough Love, Rough Love

*The difference between success
and failure is perspective.*

—Pastor Bill Towne, Jr.

"What is your definition of tough love?" I continually ask. Some answers are:

"Having principles in life and sticking to them."

"I don't cut my daughter slack anymore. She tries to control visits and I say 'No, these are my rules.' I say *when* and *if*."

"Hard. I used to give money to my daughter. Now, if she's hungry I give her something to eat. She has to get herself together. My counselor said I was an enabler."

"Sticking to your beliefs and not compromising your beliefs to someone who is strong. You need to set boundaries. You can't worry about what other people will think (friends, parents or families)."

Grandparents must establish, convey and enforce their own beliefs, boundaries, and consequences. "We cannot simultaneously set a boundary (a limit) and take care of another person's feelings. The two acts are mutually exclusive."[1] Where our sons and daughters are concerned, we have "developed a high tolerance for pain and insanity."[2] We don't want to lose them; we don't want to give up. We enable in the guise of caretaking. However, when you begin to parent grandkids, you must place their well-being above that of your son or daughter. This may eventually be your child's salvation but, in the meantime, there are difficult decisions to be made.

### Tough love

Deciding to fight for permanent custody and legal guardianship of my daughter's firstborn, Zach, was tough; walking out of the courtroom after the judge awarded it was even harder. My daughter, pregnant and pale, collapsed into the shelter of her husband's arms, while her new in-laws formed a protective circle around her. Together, they moved from the courtroom. I wanted to rush over to her, hold her, and smooth back the curls as I had done so many times when she was upset as a little girl. At the same time, I wanted to shake her when the judge asked if she would continue her son's counseling and she replied that it was a long way to drive—but "maybe a closer office." I wanted to yell at her and tell her the correct answer was "Your Honor, I'd walk on hot coals to get my son the help he needs." I wanted to cry because I "won," and I wanted *so badly* to cry because all three of us, she, myself and her son, had lost. I wanted to sink into the floor, but instead I picked up my purse and silently followed my attorney into the hall. The mind acts rationally until the heart intercedes.

## New roles for everyone

Regardless of what your grandchild calls you (and you will need to face this issue), you are no longer a functioning grandparent. Their biological mom and dad are no longer functioning parents. There is role reversal or a complete washout on the parent's part. Circumstances dictate options, but you and your grandchild must make choices.

## Legal status

You need to decide and take action! Do you want to file for legal guardianship; or for temporary, permanent or joint custody; or adopt, or do nothing? This isn't to force your child to change. It is to protect your rights and options while securing your grandchild's future. There is a strong judicial precedent for placing birth-parent rights above the best interest of the child, even after years of separation. This is especially alarming because "addiction is chronic, that is, it is constant and long lasting...addiction can also stunt a person's development."[3] Kids in grandparents' care can be difficult to raise because of early childhood neglect, abuse or abandonment. They require super, not substandard, parenting. Uprooting can be devastating. If you do nothing when you have the opportunity, you may find later that you have no options. Talk to an attorney.

## Visitations

There are lots of possibilities, endless variables, and frequent fluctuations. Generally speaking, grandparents have custody because parents are not reliable. Nevertheless, children have a right to see their birth parents (except for adopted children, who may not) as long as the parent doesn't emotionally, physically or morally put them at risk. Children's wishes are important. If they don't want to see their parents—minimize contact; if they want to see their parents—try to accommodate their wishes. Parental history, current lifestyle, future prognosis for stability, counselors' recommendations, as well as current custody, are intrinsic to all your decisions.

His blond curly hair was shaved and he looked like a miniature skinhead sitting angrily in the booster seat beside me in the car. Our bags were packed; he was going to his grandpa's for the week; I was headed back to the Midwest to visit my friend's family for New Year's. Zach had been back with me for only two weeks and, although the bruises on his little bottom and legs were fading, they weren't all gone. The bruises on his heart hadn't begun to show, let alone heal. We drove in silence for a few miles when suddenly he said in his high, little-boy voice, "My dad will be sad because he doesn't get to see me." I didn't respond and soon he repeated it. By the third time, I was frantically searching for an answer when he punched his arm in the air over his head and exclaimed in a strong voice, "But I'm glad!" Me too, sweetie, me too.

There are facilities where, for a fee, you can arrange secured observed visitations. Visits in your home should occur only if you are comfortable with the time and supervision required of you. Unsupervised visitations are appropriate when your grandchild will be safe and well taken care of whether it's for a twenty-minute walk, a two-hour basketball game, or a weekend visit.

### Conjoint parenting

It's difficult but doable. It means that both you and the birth parent act as parents. "Children and parents have the right to call themselves families, no matter how the children's time is divided."[4] With conjoint parenting your grandchild has two homes and families that "instead of competing...help stabilize life."[5] In some instances, which may include teen pregnancies, parental unemployment, or diminished mental or physical capacity, both parent and grandchild may live with you. This is up close and personal conjoint parenting! If parents relinquish their rights and responsibilities, it is like raising siblings, rather than conjoint parenting. Regardless of your living arrangements, decide who has ultimate decision-making power. Do not undermine or sabotage each other. Children are masters at manipulation given the slightest opportunity. Conjoint parenting can include extended family or friends. This gives you much-needed parenting breaks. My ex-husband took our grandson every other weekend for several years while our daughter was getting her life together. Zach now spends one weekend a month with his mom, one with his grandpa and two with me. There are three households coordinating information, holidays, schedules and problem-solving.

### Make transitions stress free

This is not a contest for control. "Parents have the right, during time spent with the children, to follow their own standards, beliefs, or style of child-raising without unreasonable interference from the other parent."[6] That's easy to say, not so easy to do. For example, I don't believe in children watching television or movies with violence, sexual content or disrespectful attitudes toward others. Media influences every area of our lives. "Their ideals become our ideals. Their thoughts become standards of our thinking and language. Their style of dress and movement is seen on the streets of our nation. And their moments of success and defeat become our successes and failures."[7] Although my daughter and my ex-husband basically agree, we draw our lines at different limits. I say no to the *Simpsons*, she says yes. I say no to *Walker, Texas Ranger* — he says yes. Zach and I talk about why I feel like I do, and why others disagree. I use differences as learning experiences. "Everyone has different rules," I tell him, "just like school rules and home rules. When you get older, you'll make your own individual rules." Then we talk about content and context — how others may have felt and how he would feel if he was the one being hit or if his son talked back to him, or if his best friend died. And we talk about how God feels.

Be flexible when you can, and be tough when you must. Drug and alcohol addicts do not consistently keep promises, remember birthdays or holidays, or maintain ongoing contact. Agreements must be changed when they aren't working, even if you end up in court. Grandkids are your first priority. Next is you. Your children come third.

## Incarceration

Parents who try to rehabilitate themselves while they are incarcerated deserve support. Parents who won't try, don't. Most state prisons have self-enrichment and family interaction programs that are voluntary, in addition to mandatory vocational or institution-maintenance jobs. County or city jail programs are more restricted. Lynn Dingle, warden at the Willow River/Moose Lake state correctional facilities, explained that in Minnesota curriculums vary. Costs, security level and design of facilities, recidivism rates, inmate demographics and type of crimes committed are factors in deciding to provide psychoeducational or family interaction programs. Classes currently include family dynamics, anger management, critical thinking skills, diversity training, tips for being a good husband or wife, or academic and technical trade education. Alcoholics Anonymous (AA), Narcotics Anonymous (NA) and sex offender treatment groups are also offered.

Religious organizations, civic groups and individual volunteers provide resources, in addition to regular personnel in prisons and halfway houses throughout the country. Girl Scouts Behind Bars helps moms in fourteen states stay in contact with their children. It "provides them with better parenting skills and heads off a generational pattern of incarceration—the girls, who range in age from five to seventeen, and their mothers work on troop projects and other activities such as aerobics or discuss family topics such as relationships."[8]

I did not take my grandson to visit his mom in prison. If Zach had been older I would have asked if he wanted to visit her and honored his decision. Jails are scary and depressing. Jail is one more piece of lost innocence for kids.

### Support

Food, clothes, insurance, transportation, allowances, child care—the list doesn't stop. Parents should pay child support; however, the reality is that most don't. Reminder: apply for a "non-needy-relative" grant through your state. This gives you several hundred dollars a month and pays for health insurance. The state seeks reimbursement from the parents, which removes the difficult task of collection from your shoulders.

### Court battles

If at all possible, try to work out differences. Tell your children what you are asking for and why. Filing petitions when all parties are in agreement is considerably cheaper than going to trial. It also leaves fewer scars and words that can't be erased.

  We will never see a miracle until we ask for one. If we say "I can do it," God will say "Go ahead."[9] This is a super time to ask for a miracle you need—to find the right words to say, both parties need receptive minds and open hearts.

  Tough love means rough choices.

—●—

Dear Zach,

  What do I say to you tonight? We went to visit your mama at the state hospital where she is staying because she's hemorrhaging. She's been there for weeks, with a guard outside her door. She's painting pictures and putting together little wooden cars for you. I'm disgusted with the state for paying the money, I'm disgusted with my daughter (your mom) for throwing you away. She was out using drugs and getting pregnant (I won't dignify it by saying "making love") with a convict on parole for armed robbery. She betrayed my trust again. I refuse to take you to jail, but thought a visit to the hospital would be okay. She went with us in her wheelchair to the parking lot and you put your hand in mine and I said, "Wave to your mom," and you did. How many times do you have to say goodbye before she'll realize what she's losing—and lost.

I'm heartsick, Zach,
Grandma

# Chapter Fourteen

# Age Daze

We each define our own restrictions.
*That's freedom.*

—Riley K. Smith and Tina B. Tessina,
*How to Be a Couple and Still Be Free*

Society, not biology, hastens old age. Sixty-five, the old-age benchmark set by Social Security as the traditional retirement age, was established when life expectancy was sixty-one-and-seven-tenths years. Today, for the average woman it is eighty-one-and-seven-tenths years and for men a little less. Twenty-eight years have been added to our lives during this century—and we mentally add them on to old age rather than spread them throughout our lifetime.

Important stuff. It took me a long time to understand that I wasn't really angry with being a mom again. Lots of people in their forties, fifties and sixties have second families; some are starting their first! What infuriated me (besides having little control over the events that precipitated my decision) was that I pictured myself at Zach's graduation and I was too old. I did not want to be old. After fifty years of responsibility, I wanted some independence and fun in my life. I wanted to help others in meaningful, self-satisfying ways, to go on religious missions to foreign countries and volunteer in prisons. I visualized being with and helping adults. It was my turn to be selfishly irresponsible or magnanimously helpful, whichever I chose. I wanted to see the Winter Olympics, tour Greece before my digestive system collapses, dance on tabletops at Senior Frogs without a walker, give new meaning to "random acts of kindness."

Instead, I'm now committed mentally and emotionally to raising my grandson. I look forward to each new day, treasuring Zach's childhood milestones and his recovery from abuse and neglect. I finally realized that I will be sixty-four when he graduates from high school, which is not all that old. Being a parent again expands, not limits, my options. I get to see Disneyland again with someone who looks out the window at mountainous dark clouds, topped with whipped-cream white ones, and a butterscotch topping of sunshine, and hear him say, "Grandma, I can see heaven!" Together or separately, my grandson and I can visit Europe, do short-term mission work, or have the freedom to decide to let someone else go. By "mom-helping" at school and at church maybe I can prevent someone from going to prison, rather than work with those already serving time. In twelve years I should still be in good health and have plenty of time to enjoy my "second retirement" from parenting. I changed career plans so I can be home more with Zach. The new path is much more invigorating than my old dreams. There is nothing to limit me but myself. I realize that grandparents who are older sacrifice much more—for them the future is today and next week and the next few years. But it may be that way for all of us. Don't delay your plans. Modify and adapt your plans, and follow through.

We use the age labels our grandparents used: teenagers, young adults, middle age, seniors and elders. We use chronological dates for bestowing rights, responsibilities and rewards: driver's license at sixteen; military draft at eighteen; legal drinking at twenty-one; over-the-hill parties at twenty-nine; retirement at sixty-five; and birthdaygrams from the President if we reach one hundred. Doctors tell us we are no longer young as soon as we hit forty. Bifocals, hormones, gray hair, yearly mammograms and sigmoidoscopies. Not much fun, but then neither were morning sickness, braces, sexually transmitted diseases, hangovers and periods. Yet no one said, "What do you expect, you're no longer a kid."

Most diseases are a result not of old age but of poor eating, exercise and lifestyle choices. "28 percent of the Medicare budget…is spent on patients who are in the final year of life."[1] Laws, advertising, employment practices and traditions have programmed us to expect poverty, sickness, and a boring life by age seventy. Today, nothing is further from reality.

Our bodies, taking orders from our minds, react to what they hear and see. Outdated stereotypes would have us sucking up prune juice instead of Gatorade. We've been programmed to expect a linear progression in life. We go to school, maybe play for a little while, get married, have babies and a career, retire, and either play or die. As baby boomers hit their fifties, paradigms are shifting. People of all generations are starting to write their own life schedules—with lots of starts, stops and sidetrips.

Generation Xers are starting their own businesses in record numbers. Corporations are hiring older workers because they are loyal, have good attendance and relate well with customers. Baby boomers are demographically the largest age group in the U.S. and experts say that they hate the idea of growing old, are self-centered, feel entitled to whatever they want or need, hate change and want quick fixes, and yet they are externally motivated, practiced protesters. Spirituality is becoming increasingly prevalent. Gerontologist Nancy Peppard claims Boomers will be "the first generation to age without maturing." I think it is exciting to be aging as part of the most powerful and youthful thinking and acting group in American history.

Happiness is a byproduct of involvement in rewarding activity. The truly happy person never has time to wonder if she is happy. I love the words of the noted modern psychiatrist, Thomas Szasz: "Happiness is an imaginary condition, formerly often attributed by the living to the dead, now usually attributed by adults to children and by children to adults." Joan Rivers said, "You can't have fun if fun is all you ever have. When every day is Sunday, Sunday doesn't exist."[2]

I didn't plan to be a mommy again. But then, I've taken lots of unplanned detours in my life. What a gift—to be given two families, two careers—a reason to get up early every morning, and a reason to keep moving toward the future. When Zach goes to college another phase of my life will just be beginning. I can't wait to see if it too turns out better than my dreams.

Faith Popcorn, trend forecaster, says we are redefining downward the definitions of age. "Forty now is what used to be thirty, fifty is now what used to be forty, sixty-five is now the beginning of the second half of life, not the beginning of the end." But the cutting edge of the trend today—and the really fun part—is not so much redefining-down as cutting loose—a sort of "let's see just how low we can go." When you raise grandchildren you are in the mainstream of youth. You and I have an edge on casting aside age stereotypes and unhealthy pessimism. My mother, now a great-grandma, never complains yet for three years she has been continually sick. She doesn't criticize and she always points out the up-side of my life. She has never given up on my daughter, nor would she let me give up. "I'm grateful for my grandchildren because otherwise I wouldn't like this part of my life. They give you something to look forward to—otherwise it could be kind of depressing," she told me the other day. Keeping up with our grandchildren will take us to new aging definitions, bring us new experiences, and keep us well grounded in our values.

—•—

Dear Zach,

You have to quit sneaking out of bed when you're at Grandpa's or Mom's and calling me at midnight. It breaks my heart to hear you whisper "Grandma, Grandma, come get me." I know you are safe, so here's the answer to your question: "Yes, I know I told you I'd come get you wherever you are if you are in trouble or need me, but when I know you are safe and just temporarily scared we'll find another solution." Didn't you feel better last night when "Nana" rubbed your back?

You are my life—but twice a month it's nice to be single and sleeping with my "other best friend," Bobby, again. He's given up so much so that I could spend these last two years working almost one-on-one with you—sometimes eighteen hours a day by the time you finally settle in. He takes you (and you alone) for breakfast and for rides in his red Corvette convertible and tells you "I'd be honored to have you for a son" when you ask him to be your dad because you "need a new daddy."

   We both love you, but give us a break!

Hugs,
Grandma

# Chapter Fifteen

# From Piggy Banks to Pensions—
# Financial Stuff

*The big print giveth
and the small print taketh away.*
—H. Jackson Brown, Jr.
*P.S. I Love You*

*Grumpy Old Men,* sequel two, take one. Charlie is sixty-eight and his friend seventy-two; both grandfathers are widowed and raising middle-school-age grandsons. As often as they can afford during the long fishing season in Washington, they load up one or the other of their old pickups and campers and head for a fishing hole. "It's more likely to happen at the beginning of the month when we get retirement and Social Security checks," says Charlie.

The two met at a grandparents' support group. "Lots of grandparents in the area can't attend," says the director. "They don't have a car and they'd spend a couple hours on the bus because the connections aren't good. Those grandparents," he continued, "really fight loneliness and isolation."

Money can be a huge issue for grandparents raising grandchildren. Two (or three or four) cannot live as cheaply as one. You'll need more money now and in the future. Your expenses are increasing while income may be flat or decreasing. Financial planning and lifestyle changes are usually essential, and may include new jobs or severe econ-omizing and innovative budgeting. Think about some of these household economics.

- Make a budget and live within it. "We can't afford it" is a complete statement.

- Consider turning a hobby into an income-producing occupation.

- Barter whenever possible.

- A sale on something you don't need is no bargain.

- Don't use ATMs that have surcharges. Open Visa accounts that have no annual fees if they offer free airline tickets or other perks. Use them, pay them off and close them. Read all fine print carefully; understand terms and obligations.

- Ask your doctor for samples of new prescriptions so you can test for side effects without spending money.

- Check with your county tax office to see if you qualify for a property tax deferral if you are a senior citizen with limited income and assets.

- Never buy clothes for children without asking, "Will you wear them?"

- Thin-sliced bread reduces the cost per serving. Creamy peanut butter goes further than chunky.

- Buy used books cheap at thrift stores and garage sales. After reading, trade them in for credit at used book stores.

- Take showers and wash your hair where you swim or work out.

- Smiles are free. ☺

- Most insurance companies give discounts to those eligible if they take a senior driving instruction class. Purchasing insurance through AARP may result in substantial savings; ask for written quotes and compare.

- For the lowest teen auto insurance rates, have grandchildren take driver's education, maintain good grades and limit driving to one vehicle.

- Keep track of stock options; mark expiration dates on your calendar.

- Combine daily walks and errands—stop at the store, post office or cleaners on your walk.

- Purchase cereal in plastic bags.

- Home merchandise parties are an expensive way to shop.

- Put leftovers in reusable containers; don't save it if it won't get eaten.

- Buy prescriptions in large quantities by mail order and save on copayments.

- Check out tax-deferred retirement and college fund account options—beware of Social Security and assistance program limits for funds in grandchildren's name.

- Music clubs offer free CDs with the purchase of one at the regular price for new members. These CDs make inexpensive gifts, but make sure you have no obligation to purchase more.

- Use credit cards for convenience only; pay them off before the due date.

- Save the cotton from aspirin and vitamin bottles for removing nail polish.

- Suggest that relatives buy U.S. government savings bonds rather than toys for your grandchildren.

- Expensive vitamins are not necessarily better vitamins.

- Buy a lipstick brush—half the lipstick is in the bottom portion of the tube.

- Purchase outgrown bicycles, athletic gear and Scouting paraphernalia from neighbors with older children.

- Don't buy fad toys—interest subsides quickly.

- Photographers offer summer specials for graduating seniors. Most use "student reps" who give out discount coupons to friends and are rewarded with dollars-off on their portraits. The same kinds of specials and discounts are available for formal wear at prom time.

- Consolidate debts using tax-deductible home mortgage loans.

- If your children use drugs, hide valuables and change the locks to your home.

- Always get a receipt for charitable donations.

- Ask if seniors and youth get reduced rates on fishing and hunting licenses.

- Custom return-address labels don't get the mail through faster.

- Sell your home yourself and save the commission. There are businesses that offer a menu of help services; e.g., appraisals, contracts, closing, advertising—each is separately priced. You select what you need.

- Buy liquor at discount stores when traveling, if it is cheaper there than where you live.

- If your house is paid off, you'll always have a place to live.

- Red convertibles cost no more than brown sedans.

- Save labels for local schools.

- Say no to phones in your grandchild's room if he or she is not responsible.

- Eliminate long distance charges by using 800 numbers or using the Internet.

- If you rent, check for damages before you move in.

- Pets are expensive. Consider food and medical costs before you purchase or accept the pet.

- Review your will at least once every two years. Leave no assets to children on drugs.

- A family can go out for pizza for less money than it takes to buy popcorn and drinks at the movies.

- Hire grandchildren for odd jobs if you own your own business. Chances are, their income is taxed at a lower rate than yours.

- Beware of battery-operated toys.

- Skip the kid's meals or better yet, the whole fast-food stop. Eat at home.

- Plant berries and vegetables in your flower beds.

- Maintain your own lawn. Clean your own house.

- Check out videos from the library rather than rent them. CDs and audiobooks are also available. Take small children to story hours.

- Give time instead of money to charity; mileage is deductible.

- Invest in an outdoor clothesline and an indoor fold-up rack.

- Liquid bleach on cement washes away moss; powdered clothes detergent with bleach works on roofs.

- Some banks and credit unions have free checking for seniors and foster parents.

- If you have a new car with manufacturer's roadside service, cancel all others.

- Ask your mechanic for new car recommendations. Compare insurance rates and gas mileage (assume the worst).

- Generic is not always cheaper.

- Keep a three- to six-month cash reserve for monthly bills.

- Pay God first; it's His money on loan to us.

- Allowances should teach grandchildren to save money, spend some on fun, and to budget for clothes, school expenses, social obligations and presents.

- Never hide valuables in your kitchen or bathroom.

- Physicals, dental check-ups and eye exams are investments—not expenses.

- Don't tip for poor service.

- Price and worth are not synonymous.

- Pay property taxes annually if there is a discount.

- "Research shows that about 75 percent of baby boomers expect to work at least part time at the end of their primary career."[1]

- Be nice to the person who cuts and colors your hair.

- Carpool, but don't forget—kids have feet!

- Take out an insurance umbrella policy if you have assets.

- Recycling saves on garbage bills and is more earth-friendly.

- Rent a small safety deposit box so you'll keep it cleaned out.

- Overdrying clothes uses energy, and wears out and shrinks garments. Take clothes out of the dryer when dry, not when it turns off.

- Be an organ donor; carry a card.

- You can check out art objects for extended periods from larger libraries.

- Some parks offer free or low-fee camping for seniors and foster parents.

- AAA offers free traveler's checks to members, as well as car rental discounts.

- Vacations are important. Take advantage of midweek and off-season rates. Cruise lines often give last-minute discounts if you can be flexible.

- Don't take the grandchildren to Disneyland unless they are tall enough to go on all the rides or small enough to fit in a stroller!

- Library cards are free.

- Skip the drive-through car wash and grab a sponge.

- Have your lawyer prepare a power of attorney document giving someone the legal authority to handle your financial affairs should you be incapacitated. Ask about custody options for your grandchildren. Make a living will outlining the kind of medical treatment you want.

- Cosign for loans for working grandchildren so they establish credit. If they don't keep up on the payments, sell the asset. Better they learn natural consequences earlier than later.

- Do not cosign for adult children who have proven themselves to be financially untrustworthy.

- Keep putting money in the retirement piggy bank.

—•—

Dear Zach,
　　Every once in awhile you try to take the little black matchbox car from my dresser. I won't let you—but it is yours when I die. You brought it home from preschool "Learning Tree" (you always called it "Learning Treat") on the day you went to live with your dad. We had taken a piñata for the kids to share and cupcakes and then it was time for me to drive you to Donald's. You took it out of your pocket and gave it to me—it was a gift from your heart and all that was left when I came back to the too quiet, too clean empty house. The most precious things in life aren't money, dear Zach.

God protect you wherever you go,
Grandma

# Chapter Sixteen

# Hugs, Healing and Happiness

*Wheresoever you go,*
*go with all your heart.*

—Confucius

Just when you were ready to retire, with no jobs and a motor home, you find yourself with two jobs and a van for carpooling. Being a full-time parent puts a different spin on everything. The good news is that the second time around, you'll probably enjoy it more. Let go of trying to be perfect and be just good enough. Letting others do for themselves reduces your stress and teaches them responsibility. Use different tactics including bribery, whining and unabashed plays for sympathy.

Capitalize on live-in excuses, such as "How can I expect the kids to fully appreciate *Barney* without that twelve-speaker surround-sound home theatre experience?" [1] "I'm sorry I can't go to the opera, Aunt Jane, but someone has to take Theodore to football practice." And "I know it's a lot of money, dear, but I needed something for myself, and this black Ferrari is it!" Your age gets you out of a lot of parental chores. "I'd like to help put up the new school playground equipment but my old back just won't let me. I'll let the young mothers go on the field trip—I've done it before." Gracious and guilt-free. We are truly blessed.

On a serious note, there is nothing wrong with a fuzzy image of a sharp concept. You know where you want to go, but be flexible about your route. Your grandchildren have often experienced more pain and ugliness than you can imagine. You may have to back up and regroup many times before you break down the barriers they have erected— barriers that have helped them survive. Admitting mistakes, apologizing and talking things over are communication skills that work. Don't bad-mouth parents but explain adamantly instead, "What happened was not right." Be authoritative, not authoritarian. Use fun and humor whenever you can. There is a lot to be learned when we stop and laugh at ourselves and the world around us. Don't give up—your grandchildren may not be able to laugh easily for a very long time.

Being a victim is not an excuse. Not for you and not for your grandchildren. I am sorry for any child who isn't raised by both biological parents. This in no way belittles or negates adoptive parents, grandparents, divorced parents, widowed parents, foster parents, stepparents, gay parents, or any other person who loves a child enough to live with the difficulties and heartache that come with raising a child. It acknowledges the deep-rooted and instinctive connectivity between child and parent. There is always, at some point in life, pain for what was lost or for what might have been. Baggage is an inevitable side effect.

"You are bound to those you love, forever and always. It doesn't matter if you argue or have serious value differences at various times in life. A family should be unbreakable."[2] I am sorry for every grandparent who comes to understand that what should be, isn't what is.

Love falters, and families break. Like molten lava, love and families reshape themselves. From destruction comes new life. If you are strong enough to survive, there will be incredible beauty and peace.

My own story continues and my daughter grows stronger daily. Both of us struggle trying to do what is best for Zach. I'm waiting for the day when it feels right to say to her, "I'm angry at you. You changed my life and almost destroyed your son." As surely as there is a God, I will be Zach's second mom forever. I will love him and protect him no less than a mother bear does her cub. Whether he calls me Mom or Grandma doesn't matter.

"Encourage others to pay back what they borrow from you, but not always to you."[3] There are many people to whom I owe a great deal. They have helped me become the person I am. I am repaying large debts in very small ways. I hope that someday your son or daughter will say to you and your grandchild, "I'm sorry." I hope you respond, "Be there for those you love. We can't go back—let's go forward." It's funny how sometimes the gift we give turns out to be the gift we receive.

——•——

Dear Zach,

"It's okay to judge, but don't criticize," says our pastor. As you grow older you'll have to sort through lots of feelings, stories and past experiences. Never think of yourself as a victim—you aren't. You have the advantage of knowing pain so you can help others.

I love your laugh. It was silent for a long time so I stop and smile whenever I hear it. When you are dating, always, always, always respect yourself, your date and the little souls up in heaven who are waiting for you to someday be their daddy. No matter what you do or where you go, our hearts will be connected. Years ago, I was told by an astrologer that April 8 (your birthday) would be important to me. It was—you've changed my life—and for that I will always be grateful.

Love,
Your second mom and maternal grandma,
Joan Callander

# Notes

## Chapter One
1. Description given by state caseworker.
2. Dave Thomas, *Well Done! The Common Guy's Guide to Everyday Success* (Grand Rapids: Zondervan Publishing House, 1994), p. 129.

## Chapter Two
1. Gary Smalley and John Trent, *The Two Sides of Love* (Pomona: Focus on the Family, 1990), p. 7.

## Chapter Five
1. Conversation with my sister, Judy Biggs, spring 1998.
2. Dan Sullivan, *The Great Crossover* (Toronto: Strategic Coach, 1994), p. 57.

## Chapter Six
1. Thomas, *Well Done! The Common Guy's Guide to Everyday Success,* p. 63.

## Chapter Seven
1. Carole T. Guinta, "Fetal Alcohol Syndrome," (short Internet version ) in *Social Casework: The Journal of Contemporary Social Work.*
2. Thom Hartman, *Attention Deficit Disorder: A Different Perception* (Grass Valley: Underwood, 1993).
3. Hartman, pp. 82-86.
4. Sylvie de Toledo and Deborah Edler Brown, *Grandparents as Parents* (New York: Guilford, 1995), p. 96.

5.  Harold S. Koplewica, *It's Nobody's Fault* (New York: Times Books, 1996), p. 73.
6.  Stanley I. Greenspan, *The Challenging Child* (Reading: Addison-Wesley, 1995), p. 16.
7.  Robert Karen, "Becoming Attached," in *Atlantic Monthly,* February 1990, p. 62.
8.  Christine Portland, "Symptoms of Character Disturbed, in Unattached Children," (manuscript).
9.  *Diagnostic and Statistical Manual of Mental Disorders,* fourth edition (American Psychiatric Association).
10. Rebecca Perbix Mallow, "Trauma and Attachment," in *Family Matters Newsletter,* Special Needs Adoption Coalition, Boys and Girls Aid Society of Oregon, June/July 1997, p. 2.

## Chapter Eight

1.  Ann Landers, *The Quotable Woman* (Philadelphia: Running Press), p. 183.
2.  S. Robert Lichter, Linda S. Lichter and Stanley Rothman, *Watching America* (New York: Prentice-Hall, 1991), p. 9.
3.  *Safeguarding Your Children* (Chicago: National PTA, 1995).
4.  Margit Feury, "Family Meals Heal," in *Family Circle,* Feb. 1, 1998, p. 57.
5.  de Toledo and Brown, *Grandparents as Parents,* p. 128.
6.  Spencer Johnson, *The One-Minute Father* (New York: Candle Communications, 1983), p. 15–25.
7.  Johnson, p. 24.

## Chapter Nine

1. Hallmark 1998 quotation calendar, February 3.
2. Soundtrack from *Pocahontas,* a Walt Disney production.
3. *The Reader's Digest Legal Question and Answer Book* (Pleasantville: Reader's Digest Association, 1988), p. 88.
4. "HIV Negative" (Research Triangle Park, North Carolina: American Social Health Association, 1994).
5. "HIV/AIDS" (Research Triangle Park, North Carolina: American Social Health Association, 1991).
6. "HIV Negative." *The Reader's Digest Legal Question and Answer Book,* p. 92.
7. Deborah Ducette-Dudman and Jeffrey R. LaCure, *Raising Our Children's Children* (Minneapolis: Fairview Press, 1996), p. 10.

## Chapter Ten

1. Jan Wagner, *Not My Child!* (Yellow, Texas: Dino Publishing,1994).
2. Dan Hurley, "Lost and Found," in *Family Circle,* Sept. 15, 1998, p. 47.
3. Hurley, p. 47.
4. "Safeguarding Your Children" (Chicago: National PTA, 1995).

## Chapter Twelve

1. Laura Schlessinger, *Ten Stupid Things Women Do to Mess Up Their Lives* (New York: Villard, 1994), pp. 40-41.

2.   Peter McWilliams and John-Roger McWilliams, *Life 101* (Los Angeles: Prelude Press, 1990), p. 99.

## Chapter Thirteen
1.   Melody Beattie, *Beyond Codependency* (San Francisco: Harper & Row, 1989), p. 174.
2.   Beattie, p. 172.
3.   de Toledo and Brown, *Grandparents as Parents*, p. 117.
4.   Christine Portland, "Conjoint Parenting Agreement: An Agreement as to What Children Need," Portland, 1997.
5.   Iolina Ricci, *Mom's House, Dad's House* (New York: Macmillan, 1980), p. 111.
6.   Portland.
7.   Jodie Foster, speaking for American Film Institute, CBS, June 16, 1998.
8.   "Girl Scouts Promote Parenting from Behind Bars," in *Corrections Professional*, Mar. 21, 1997, p. 5.
9.   From a sermon by Pastor Bill Towne, Jr., Rolling Hills Church, Portland, Oregon, January 1998.

## Chapter Fourteen
1.   Ken Dychtwald and Joe Flowers, *Age Wave* (New York: G. P. Putnam's Sons, 1989), p. 79.
2.   Joan Rivers, *Bouncing Back* (New York: Harper-Collins, 1977), p. 111.

## Chapter Fifteen
1.   Gail Sheehy, author of *New Passages: Mapping Your Life across Time*, quoted in *Hope Publications Newsletter*, International Health Awareness Center.

## Chapter Sixteen

1. Chelsea Audio/Video, "Helpful Guide to Rationalization," 1998.
2. Estée Lauder (New York: Random House, 1985), p. 96.
3. Thomas, *Well Done!*, p. 212.

# Index

To order additional copies of

# Second Time Around